the journey's the thing

the journey's the thing

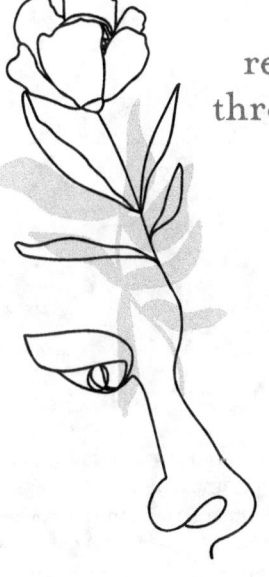

reflections on healing
through the written word

dera nevin

Q!

QUENTIN IMPRINTS
NEW YORK CITY, NEW YORK

THE JOURNEY'S THE THING
Quentin Imprints, New York, NY

Editing, proofreading, cover design, and interior book design provided by Indigo: Editing, Design, and More:

    Line editor: Cooper Lee Bombardier
    Proofreaders: Kristen Hall-Geisler and Jenn Kepler
    Cover designer: Olivia Hammerman
    Interior book designer: Vinnie Kinsella

www.indigoediting.com

Library of Congress Control Number: 2025920493

ISBN 979-8-9876460-2-1
eISBN: 979-8-9876460-3-8
Audiobook ISBN: 979-8-9876460-4-5

For those with whom we traveled.
For those that walked beside us and before us.
For those that carried us.
For those we left behind.

Contents

Introduction

Twelve minutes a day.

Every day, for a year.

Each morning, I'd wake up early, often before sunrise. I'd boil water and make myself a pot of tea. The package instructions were clear: Let the tea steep for a full twelve minutes. So I'd set a timer, pick up a pen, and write.

Each Monday I'd think of a word and write it at the top of a page. Then I'd write whatever came to mind about that topic. I'd keep writing each morning on that theme until Sunday. By the end of the week, each of those twelve-minute segments would add up to an essay. And the next day, Monday, I'd write a new and different word at the top of another page.

I started this ritual in a moment of personal crisis, during a time when nothing in my life was working out as planned, and everything was just...hard. I was grieving the deaths of close family members and working through life-altering changes after the loss of a primary relationship, when I found myself suddenly in a small basement apartment in New York City's Upper West Side. I had just taken a new job that was unreasonably stressful, and I was recovering from a serious illness. Then the pandemic hit, and suddenly I had two friends in the hospital on ventilators.

The world turned upside down, and everything and everyone around me went crazy. My neighborhood was emptied of people and toilet paper, leaving behind only the sounds of sirens and seagulls. I was completely alone.

I was putting one word after another, the same way that people carry on when things get tough by putting one foot in front of the other. While everything seemed to have been taken away, I was trying to write my way into clarity, process everything that was going on in my head and heart, and get it out in the world to maintain my mental health.

I didn't know it at the time, but those twelve minutes day after day would change everything for me. The essays reflect the changes I underwent during this time and are a testament to the effectiveness of consistent journaling practice. I discovered that mindful journaling improved my work-life balance, helped me better manage my everyday stress, and maintained my mental health. Daily writing was also a journey of self-improvement for me, as I worked through my goals, my faith and spiritual practice, and my personal meaning of a good life.

After a few weeks, I started to rework the essays and post the slightly edited versions to my private social media, mostly for accountability. Although I wasn't sure that anyone would read them, I could imagine that there would be some sort of record if I stopped writing, and this would be motivating for me.

What I didn't anticipate was the reaction. Posting week after week opened connections with others and conversations I didn't expect yet nourished me and deepened friendships. I was told repeatedly by others how sustaining the essays were, and how they inspired them to start their own journaling practice. It turns out that although writing may be a solo practice, it is a team sport. Both the process and the outcome are improved by sharing with trusted friends.

Twelve minutes a day. Together, let's begin that journey now.

On Starting

I've just entered my fiftieth year. I've often observed my birthday by making resolutions, and this year is no exception, despite the alien and solo experience of it as we remain in pandemic lockdown. For this final revolution around the sun in my forties, I've resolved to write fifty reflective essays. I'm calling this unfolding "Fifty for Fifty."

That I am starting this journey at all is the victory. It's true I am a notorious starter of things: projects, adventures, chores, companies, travels, and errands. But it's also true I do not always follow through on many of the things I start. I quit, and I quit often and a lot. Usually, I quit because I get bored. Sometimes, too, I start so many things that I get overwhelmed, lose focus, and panic as I sense the proverbial balls dropping. I enjoy the adrenaline rush I get from a blastoff, that dopamine hit that satisfies my need for acceleration. I get inspired by having lots going on, and I acknowledge that speed is a substitute for engagement at depth. I often wallow in shame when I think of so many half-completed and abandoned projects and, in certain moods, can dust off the crumbs of half-baked ideas and overdramatize the purported failures of what might have been.

The starting of a *writing* project, though, is not a difference in degree for me; it's a difference in kind. Writing is perhaps *the thing* I have most longed to do but have neglected, and too frequently and deliberately failed to start. If you had asked me as a child what I wanted to be when I grew up, I would have said "a journalist, a writer." If I divide my expected life span of seventy-five years into rough thirds, I see that in those first twenty-five years I wrote all the time: poems, stories, diary entries, essays, even a play or three. I surrounded myself with magazines and newsprint and books and type. Even during my college years, I consistently took creative writing courses, published several poems and stories, and created multiple broadsheets, journals, and chapbooks.

However, I've now spent much of the second third of my life racked by guilt and grieving about not writing while simultaneously living in fear of writing, resulting in a peculiar affliction of a psychic phantom limb. I've tried to understand why I do this. Sometimes I pretend it's a failure of will or character: I imagine I discontinued writing from fear or family loyalty, because my mother and I used to have screaming matches about my intended vocation, with her crying hysterically that if I took up writing, I'd be flirting with poverty, rejection, and disaster. Or I'd imagine myself to be insufficiently resilient to write "for real" when I remember the emotional injuries I've sustained from criticism I received over some early efforts. (In hindsight, I see this was not particularly good work.) In these moments I am not generous with myself, for at other times I acknowledge that I am also just busy.

And that I can also rationalize to myself that I *have* spent that period writing, just related to my job as a lawyer. Over the past two decades, I've written a textbook, briefs for court, thousands of pages of policy, and a column that was published for years. But I concede that I have not set aside the time nor devoted the focus that *writing as my heart's desire* might merit. And, despite writing a lot, I have not identified myself as a writer or creative person, perhaps to let myself off the hook so I don't look too deeply at why I'm denying myself the experience of writing for pleasure.

So now, rounding into the third third of my life, to commit to a process of writing that is not journaling is an indulgence for me from me—a gift. As my pandemic project, I'll be writing essays, using them to imagine into what I want my next decade to become. Through this process, I am reclaiming dormant aspects of my identity and living into inspiration.

I hope you enjoy reading these essays as much as I am going to enjoy the process of writing them. Because now, in this final sentence of the first essay, we're beyond the starting of the thing and into the time for follow-through. We are on the journey itself.

On Staying

I'm staying. Despite the many reasons to leave New York City, I'm staying. That's the decision I made this weekend—or rather, a statement I said aloud to a friend as we were rounding the north side of the Jackie O. Reservoir in Central Park on a morning walk. We were cataloging various people we both know: where they are and what they may be doing come September or in the new year. So many people we know are leaving the city for Connecticut, New Jersey, or elsewhere.

But I said: "I'm staying."

I said these words of commitment right near the spot where, on June 9, 2014, I'd resolved I was going to move to New York. The north end of the Jackie O. seems to be a spot of declaration for me, where I can look south and see the Chrysler Building and Billionaires' Row standing at attention in Midtown. There's something about this view that helps me to be certain. And now that it's declared, it's decided—because there's a power in such moments. In that spot six years ago, I decided, *I'll move to NYC*, and less than three months later, I was here. And then, six years later, in almost the same spot, I decide that I'll stay, despite this crisis of the pandemic.

I've loved the idea of New York City even before I came here from my hometown of Toronto for the first time, and I loved the city itself after I started to visit. I loved it when I decided to move here, when I welcomed friends and visitors here, when times were terrible and when they were better. But loving New York City when you are not from here, when most of your life has been somewhere else, is complicated.

I love the press of people, the movement, and the variety of the city. I love the hustle, reinvention, and innovation, as well as the seediness, the stench, and the other aromas. I love that everyone has somewhere to go, somewhere to be, and something to do, and I love its worn-down subway system that goes both everywhere and nowhere. Its hole-in-the-wall restaurants that serve the best food I've ever eaten. The roughed-up sidewalks that would have stories to tell if they could talk. Street vendors for everything. Every language. Every story. Everyone here to compete with the best for the ultimate prize: a new self. This city *is* the American dream, the American promise.

I even have patience for the city's idiocies, like the throwaway five-dollar umbrellas that magically appear on every corner the minute it rains. The constant petty thievery and fraud and corruption. The stench of garbage and the unbearable humidity in the summer. The water bugs and rats everywhere. Watching the trucks lift air conditioners into the top floors of swanky apartments every April. The absurd cocktail prices in bars on the Lower East Side. The unending train ride to the edges of Brooklyn, the Bronx, and Queens.

I declared I'm staying in this city even though for others it's departure time. I constantly see moving trucks taking possessions away, but no second moving truck ushering someone else in. I know people are asking more and more questions: How will I survive? (*I can't pay rent*, he says, or *It's me, my husband, and two kids I need to homeschool in this tiny apartment*, she says.) Why am I here? (*Now that I am working from home, and it's likely to be permanent*, he asks.) How will I live? (*I need more quiet; I need time to recenter and focus on my projects*, she says.) I understand their desire to leave. I have thought many times myself about leaving during these claustrophobic days of the pandemic, when fear and sadness grip the city.

But I'm staying. My continuing desire to remain here is a revelation for me. It was a rough few months here during the spring. It's been heartbreaking to see the stages dark, museums empty, and all neon off. Midtown is emptied of people. Stores are shuttering. There are empty seats on the subway and on buses. Pigeons are lean, dazed. As the crushing heat and humidity of the city's summer settles in, there's a low, slow pitch of desperation, and some of the economic dislocation frays at the fabric of life.

There's a lot in and of the city to grieve, and we may still be in some shock over what we've just seen and lived through this past spring. A mass grave less than two miles away as the crow flies. There was a field hospital a half mile from me. A hospital ship docked on the Hudson River. Bodies in bags in freezer trailers on Randalls Island and elsewhere across the city because the second line of defense—morgues—could not keep up. Kids without meals because they aren't in school. A fear so palpable it transmitted through the air like a second wave of contagion entwined with the virus. Mad scrounges for toilet paper. Freezers in supermarkets completely emptied of food. Sirens. Sirens. Sirens for days on end, sirens without end. A morning walk in a light drizzle in the gloaming of early April, crossing the street as a lone male in scrubs shuffles down the sidewalk, possessed by a look of desperation and exhaustion. I could not even imagine what he'd just seen, what he will see.

Yet there have been shattering moments of beauty and community. That's why I'm staying. I remember when, one morning in mid-April, there were a thousand newly minted runners trying the loop of Central Park. I welcomed them silently. I've run that loop hundreds of times every year that I've been here. If I hadn't tired of it in the past couple of months when it was the only thing I'd seen, it was unlikely I'd ever tire of it. Of course I'm staying, and I should have known I'm staying because at the critical moment of crisis, I stayed. When the pandemic first arrived, I thought I stayed because where else would I have gone? But I see now that I stayed because I have everything I need and what I want here. I've built a life for myself, and I knew I'd be safer here—physically, mentally, and spiritually—than anywhere else. Central Park is both my witness and my anchor.

I was in the Ramble in Central Park the moment when Amy Cooper called the police on a Black male birdwatcher. I was in Central Park a week later, helicopters overhead, reading about the new curfew on my phone, both angered and terrified. I was in the Ramble again when I heard distant chanting growing louder and realized I'd be cut off by a massive march along Central Park West before an 8:00 p.m. curfew. But I also stood in Central Park many nights during the spring and summer at 7:00 p.m. as the cacophony of pots, trombones, and clapping started. I've found refuge in Central Park under cherry blossoms when the death toll was consistently over seven hundred souls a day, and grieved, crying hot tears. I have emerged from the Shakespeare Garden and been delighted by gatherings of families having picnics on blankets. In Central Park, I've cheered strangers getting married, reunited with my running buddies, gone for looping walks around its perimeter, made friends with cardinals, meditated beside a waterfall, and watched baby ducklings grow. This is my little part of New York City, and I know that outside this oasis of green, the rest of the Manhattan waits for me.

So, I'm staying. At least I can say that for now, because this is New York City and nothing in New York City can be permanent, not even the city itself.

On Comparing

I've noticed I've been comparing myself to others recently. Perhaps I am more immersed in social media during this time of pandemic isolation than I was before. Comparing, I've discovered, is among the most self-destructive of my habits of mind, and the one that invites the most suffering. Whether by observing how others present themselves on social media (or how I imagine them to be) or by being my own worst backseat driver during this time of ennui and examining my life from the delusional perspective of a thousand roads not taken, comparing drains my energy and robs me of joy in where I am right now.

I tend to engage in comparing when I am tired and emptied of reserves. Instead of allowing myself gentleness, gratitude, and rest, I use the act of comparing to flagellate myself with either a "could have" or "should have" simply by imaging how, if I had made different choices, I'd feel better or be better, in the sense that things would be closer to some ideal. Which ideal or whose ideal, I can't tell you, but in my imaginings it's the one that leaves me less tired, less exhausted, less feeling wanting, and less alienated.

I look at where I am, what I have, who I am, and think: *Is this enough? Am I doing it right? What am I missing?* I imagine I'm wasting time, talent, and energy, and that others have more happiness, more joy, more fruitful relationships and careers, or that they have hewed closer to their guiding stars, that they somehow have this exercise called life more figured out than I do.

I can wallow in such feelings and become enmeshed in stories: if I were born wealthier or to better parents; if I had studied more or gone to a more prestigious school; if I had stayed in this relationship or that job; if I had taken a different set of risks or saved rather than spent. If I had only settled down, traveled more, traveled less, been more open with people, been less open with people. If I had been someone else and done different things, everything would be different! I'd be married, have more money, have a house, have a career. You name it—in my imaginings I can invent an outcome I don't currently have by rearranging the board. That I don't ordinarily act in ways that could result in any of those "ideals" is not what I consider when I find myself comparing. Neither do I acknowledge whether any imagined failing would be an authentic expression of me, or that where I am exactly now is the best manifestation of who and how I am, because that is, in fact, who and how I am.

These kinds of acts of comparing lack gratitude and realism, and thus also lack courage, honesty, and trust. Comparing oneself to ideals not faithfully held is the opposite of surrender. Comparing has fear and a miscalibration of risk at its root. No grace is possible in a state of comparing.

I remind myself to contrast comparing with discerning. To compare is to look for the differences between two or more things, to emphasize differences over similarities.

To discern is to detect with the senses, to come to know or recognize, to identify as separate and distinct. The difference between these is subtle and requires discernment itself. Both involve separation and distinction, but one is an effort to separate; the other is understanding that separateness exists. Discernment envelops and celebrates uniqueness; it has an affect of grace, even celebration.

I often resolve feelings of comparing by connecting, because that's the opposite of the separating and distinguishing that comparison requires. Connecting with people puts me in conversation and in community. Connecting with nature or movement puts me in flow. Connecting with my breath—whether through meditation, running, or walking—puts me back in my body and away from the isolation of my mind. All of these actions reinforce me *here*, doing this and only this, which roots me, even within an acknowledgment of imperfection. It reminds me that every moment is an opportunity to learn, to discern, and to connect. Anything and everything that happened is in the past and shapes me but does not define me. What defines me is only what I do next, and how I show up in the next moment, not only what I have been but also what I am being and what I am becoming.

It reminds me, too, that I am more alike others than different from them. Everyone else, too, is exactly who they are now, between a bundle of history and an unfolding of possibility.

Here and now, doing this and only this. It's actually all that any of us have. Here and now is everything, and that's enough.

On Deciding

My closest friends know that I can be indecisive. If I invite them for a walk when I'm in one of my moods, I'm trying to work through a waffle and use walking and talking to lubricate decision-making. I can overanalyze and spend too much time on research. I can ask too many people for their opinions and delay a decision by seeking second, third, and fourth opinions. I can prepare charts, make decision trees as a substitute for making a decision, or just lie in bed in the dark for hours with the decision wheel endlessly spinning in my mind. I have stretched out simple decisions for months, even years.

Sometimes I break through my indecisiveness with apparent recklessness, in the sense that despite thinking over the issues, I can't trace the series of thoughts that carried the decision. My decision to move to New York was like that; I contemplated moving out of Toronto for over ten years and kept on circling the idea of New York, and then just like that, I decided to move there. It was a decision made quickly, in slow motion.

Sometimes I break paralysis by following the crowd. Or I just take any action, even one I suspect at the time may not be a good one, just to move into something other than waffling. After I make such a decision, I can review the minutiae of what happened until my feelings morph into regret. Or my analysis paralysis can take over to the point that I analyze my analysis. This can get exceptionally *meta*.

I've been reflecting consistently on this tendency of mine during the lockdown. I see that my indecisiveness arises from avoidance. I am indecisive because I don't know what I want or won't admit what I do want to myself or to others. If you don't know where you want to go, any road will get you there. So will taking no roads at all. In this way, waffling is also related to and arises from fear. I fear that things will not work out the way I imagine, and so I try to put off that disappointment by avoiding a decision.

A friend is wrestling with whether to leave New York and move to another state to be closer to family. His lease renewal is due, and this pushes him toward deciding. He works and reworks all possibilities and explores all avenues: Do I stay in this apartment? Do I stay in NYC? Do I move? Possibilities are analyzed and weighed. I try not to get frustrated, because these are important decisions for him, and really, I am not frustrated with him but at a reflection of myself that is being held up for me to see. Too often what frustrates us in others is what lies unacknowledged and unloved within ourselves.

In our discussions, to stop him from spinning, I say, "There's no perfect decision, only a good one." By this I mean: you can analyze everything, but there are infinite criteria and infinite possibilities. If you don't know what you want, you won't be able to determine whether any possibility meets your criteria. And in any event, life isn't and can't be perfect, and so no decision can be perfect either.

We can only make the best decisions we can, with the information, feelings, and capabilities that we have now.

To decide is always a form of violence, a mini-death. To decide is to commit deicide, killing the god, killing possibility. By deciding, we eliminate one potential pathway in favor of another. We don't walk down that one road not taken, but we do walk down another. In so doing, the doors that might have been opened by that other road may remain closed, those possible outcomes forgone forever. Yet other doors and possibilities may open to us on the road we are taking. We lose one world, but we gain another.

I see so consistently the relationship between deciding and action, and between fear and avoidance, and how fear and deciding cannot coexist for me. The intermediary, what helps me move through the decision, is feelings—specifically, the ability to recognize and face fear or other powerful emotions. Fear especially needs to be right-sized, because not feeling the right amount or right kind of fear contributes to avoidance, which can manifest as decision paralysis, or "freezing."

My running avocation has blessed me with damaged toenails. Despite my best efforts to take care of them, the nails on the long second toes (my toes are unusual in this configuration) can split or splinter and are susceptible to becoming ingrown. The nails are quite thick, don't cut well, and generally I find it hard to take care of them. For this reason, and for the pure pleasure of it, I'm usually an enthusiastic consumer of nail salons. I haven't been to a nail salon since February, even though they have started to reopen with precautions in place in Manhattan.

This weekend, I tried to cut my toenail and it split. Earlier in the day I had been on a very long run and could feel my toenails hitting the tops of the toe boxes of my shoes. Something had to be done, and here I was trying to do something, not particularly successfully. I was waffling on going to the nail salon through a risk lens, although I had just passed by the salon and knew it was empty. And I wanted to go. I missed the experience and being around humans. I looked closely at what was really going on, and I realized it wasn't fear that was the barrier; it was shame. I was ashamed of the way my feet looked, but I was also ashamed of needing to be around other people, of being too vulnerable. Yet I needed to be around other humans because I don't have enough real contact with people. I also needed someone to pamper me a little bit, because I also haven't been taking care of myself. With my understanding of all of that, the decision to leave my house and go to the nail salon became easier, because I could pinpoint what difficult emotions needed to be processed and why. Now, after my salon visit, I can look down and see my lovely painted-azure-blue toenails to remind me of my decision.

Instead of waffling in indecision and how it might not work out the way you expect or anticipate, relish the opportunity to decide. For every fork in the road, take it. Rejoice that for every road not traveled, there is a road that *is* traveled. Perhaps, too, things will work out better than you imagined, and there is freedom and grace in taking a decision and trying. A life worth living is one in which forks in the road of life's journey are endlessly encountered and experienced. I continue to learn that decisions are gifts, opportunities for self-expression, personal growth, and unfolding. And each good-enough decision I make, whether big or small, consequential or massive, unfolds my unique path on this earth.

On Running

Inevitably with me, one gets to running. I started running as a child, and to this day I run. Running, along with writing, has been a constant in my life. I don't run every day, but I do run often. I ran this morning, hot loopy miles around Midtown Manhattan, hugging the perimeter of the city. I no longer run fast, and I don't always run with enthusiasm or grace, but I do run with constancy and consistency.

In primary and middle school, I found purpose and direction in short-distance track and the long jump. In high school I found confidence on the cross-country team, and as an 800m specialist. Running grounded me and kept me sane in my twenties. I remember starting to take recreational training seriously and investing for the first time in proper footwear: the Nike Pegasus. I lived in Kingston, Ontario, a city of universities, military bases, and prisons, and I'd run evenings out past Kingston Penitentiary and up to a neighboring town of Cataraqui. Mornings I'd head east over the causeway past Fort Henry, sometimes timing my runs with the sunrise. On August evenings, I'd wait for thunderstorms, grab my shoes, and run through puddles in the middle of the street.

While in law school, I joined Running from the Law, a running club of law students, and I returned to the north Toronto loops I had not run since high school: up Avenue Road and through the ravines back to the University of Toronto. A law school friend suggested I try a road race, which I did not finish. The boyfriend of a law school roommate pushed me to run farther and try a half-marathon, which became my favorite distance. I started to log miles. While articling (an internship for lawyers in Canada), I decided to train for my first marathon because, of course, why not do two hard things at once, for *balance*?

One Sunday I showed up at the office, and my mentor and articling principal was astonished to learn I had run fourteen miles that morning.

"That's out to Scarborough and back!" he exclaimed. Scarborough is a suburb of Toronto.

"That's exactly what I did," I replied. And then that afternoon I wrote a twenty-page legal research memo.

Over the next decade, a dedicated crew of friends and athletes brought out the best runner in me, helping me often through sixty- to ninety-mile weeks while I maintained a brutal litigation practice at work. I learned to love "the double," running speed intervals on the track in the morning and easy miles in the evening, often late after long workdays. My half-marathon time fell below ninety minutes. My 10K fell below forty minutes and my 5K below nineteen minutes. That speed never translated to the marathon, but I didn't give up. Through perseverance and practice, I qualified for, and ran my fastest time ever, at the Boston Marathon. In my late thirties, I won a (small) marathon.

But I had little balance. I was running big miles and working bigger hours. I was often injured or just sore. I was tired and constantly freezing. I could not keep weight on. Thinking I had an eating disorder, a group of friends intervened. Their planned intervention coincided with a Saturday evening dinner at home where I literally ate an exceptionally large bowl of pasta and a tub of vanilla ice cream in front of them. I didn't have an eating disorder; instead, my metabolism was in overdrive. Eventually, I stepped back the training, focusing instead on relearning running mechanics and working hard to—literally—slow down so I would cease being injured all the time.

When I arrived in New York City, I took sightseeing runs to explore my new home. I entered local races as an excuse to visit new places. I tried to coordinate vacations with random races. This got me running in Delaware, Pennsylvania, California, Tennessee, and South Dakota. I got slower and thicker around the waistline, and I wasn't always cold.

But during this time, running still grounded me and pushed me forward. It was on a run, after all, that I had decided to move to New York City. Running helped me heal a broken heart and work through complicated feelings when I learned that a good friend from whom I had become estranged had died. I run in every city I visit on vacation or for work; this avocation has given me eyes on the whole world.

Running has gifted me extraordinary friendships and remarkable connections. There is something about the shared activity of moving side by side that deepens vulnerability and opens hearts. Even when my friends do not themselves run, they have chosen to share in my love for this sport, come to see me at races, met me after training sessions, and just generally been supportive. The solitude of the long-distance runner is not a myth, but it is excessively romanticized. We are pack animals, and running proves this out. I am grateful for my sweaty, sometimes stinky running tribe.

I don't believe I am exaggerating when I say that no activity has given me more experiences and friendships, nor built up and revealed my character, than running has. It's strange, then, that I don't define myself only as a runner, but also as someone who runs. My identity is bound up both in *doing* running as an activity and in *being* a runner.

Because it's also true that I have a penchant for movement beyond the activity of running, and not infrequently I just drop everything and, well, move, usually by running. I am not really one for staying still. If I am not running, I'll often just walk, or get up and move. Or fidget. I can get anxious and misdirect energy with too much inertia—and I need to feel less inertia (or more *ertia*) than most. I move apartments. I move jobs. I prefer things to move fast, and I can grow impatient with stillness. I am constantly running away from aspects of my life that I don't like or that bore me, or running toward something that interests or excites me. I run to avoid anxiety, and I run to induce excitement. I run to escape feelings of my own limitations or inferiority. I run to push past my boundaries and see what I can do. And I run to move away from what I experience as restrictive. Sometimes I run to push against my own mortality, and my fear of being hurt or dying. I run to push against time, and I run to test time. Running expands me yet highlights my boundaries. It gifts me my edges against the world: my experiences, companions, and relationships.

So, I'm someone who runs. I'm proud of it and defined by it. I look forward to many more years of running in the decades to come, and I know I will continue to be enriched by running and the people it brings into my life. Who knows whom I'll have met by the end of this racecourse I call my life, but I know I will be glad and grateful for their miles when I cross my final finish line.

On Belonging

(or Why I Love The Little Prince)

Today while meditating during a run, it occurred to me that I'm a stray. It's a metaphor, of course, for my perception of my lived experience. This thought may have been prompted by a TV show I watched last night about a man who finds stray and shelter dogs forever homes. He's easy to look at, and the dogs are adorable, and who doesn't want a happy ending for all. The show traffics on everyone's need for belonging.

Belonging means "an affinity for a place or situation." It is associated with the human need to give and receive attention. When we belong, we experience belongingness, the emotional need to be an accepted member of a group, whether it is family, friends, coworkers, a religion, or some other group. People have an innate human need to be associated with something greater than themselves. Belonging is the antidote to loneliness and isolation.

Belonging, and experiencing belongingness, is a primary emotional need, one that undergirds our mythologies and much-received wisdom expressed as culture: stories of belonging are the stories we tell ourselves. And we tell stories to facilitate and cement belonging. As much as belonging feels like security and peace, it arises from a sense that one is connected to others in a way that creates order. Stories are the glue for that order. We belong, in some sense, when we know—and can accept in our hearts—those stories that will be told about us by others in the group.

In Western culture, the family is the primary unit of belonging. We experience belonging when our families reflect to us an image of ourselves that we accept and can grow into. Belonging helps crystalize identity and self-identity; we can become ourselves only as and when we see ourselves reflected in another's eyes. Although I have a biological family, my family doesn't actually function as one. Since I was young, my father has been absent, not only physically but also emotionally; he is simply unable to interrelate. My mother was, gently speaking, untethered to reality. It is not possible to belong, except in an abstract sense, to the absent and the insane.

So, I became a stray. I found surrogate families, many of which have contributed to my present self-perception. They have been wonderful and have taken me in and helped me heal when I was broken, or have granted me refuge or companionship, and gifted me joy and laughter. But none of these have stuck. I continue to roam as a stray.

My perception of being a stray has certainly impacted my conception of "home." I have a perversity for moving; having a lightness of physical infrastructure has enabled me to cycle through various homes and places. Because I am accustomed to not feeling an affinity for a place or situation, I have been able to keep moving. My restlessness arises when I have a difficult time staying put in a location and feeling it to be home. While I often profess that "if I just bought a house" or "just redecorated" I'd feel more at home, I know that these physical places in which I live are not substitutes for belonging. My itchy feet may be code for "I feel no belongingness."

To be a stray, then, involves an uncertain relationship with becoming tamed. I am imperfectly tamed in the sense that I have a limited coherent self-identity.

This insight, achieved during today's run, brought into focus why I've always loved the book *The Little Prince*. He, too, is a stray, tamed by his flower. In the gulf of isolation on his little planet, he first seeks belonging by tending to his baobabs. However, despite finding his beloved flower and achieving a purpose by tending to her, he leaves and goes on adventures. I had always thought that the little prince and I shared a thrill of travel and wanting to see the world, and that's why I loved the book. That's not it; I realize it speaks to me because it's a guide to the challenges of achieving belonging when one isn't (fully) tamed.

On Earth, while the little prince meets the pilot—also a stray, but one with a strong sense of belonging through family, friends, and a connection to the war—he recounts the tension of the stray. The adventures he tells to the pilot are about the struggle to belong.

The fox that the little prince meets on his travels is an advocate for seeking an orderly taming by an external actor or force and describes the development of trust and belonging from routine: the fox thinks that perhaps the prince, the boy with the flaxen hair, will tame the fox by appearing at the same time every day, allowing him to develop trust in the routine. The fox will come closer as the trust develops. Trust is essential to belonging, but for those who do not have the foundations of self-identity through belonging, the risk is that they will substitute the control occasioned by showing up for another for belonging. In extremes, codependency, cults, acute fandom, demagoguery, and denial can create this sense of belonging.

The snake that the prince searches out to return him to his beloved flower is an advocate for finding belonging through dissolution—literally and metaphorically, in the prince's case, through death. The prince tells himself the story that when his little planet with his flower is directly overhead, he can be reunited with his love without his body. The snake's bite cautions us against finding belonging in internally developed and imposed delusions, in fantasies that are not grounded in their objects.

In times of turbulence, such as the ones in which we presently live with a pandemic uprooting so many aspects of our lives, relationships, and routines, aren't we all at risk of becoming strays? When our sense of belonging is attenuated, will we be seduced by the illusions of being tamed by the fox's order, or seek out dissolution in the snake's bite? Or do we remember our physical connection to our flowers, our need to tend and water them daily and protect them from drafts? Can we honor those flowers, even though we have left them and are wandering in the desert in a foreign land? Can those connections help us see with correct eyes a story on which we can agree, whether it's a hat or, as the little prince would have it, a snake eating an elephant?

We all need to belong; it's a foundational human emotion. But we truly belong when we are reflected honestly by others and become more deeply and inextricably ourselves through an affinity with a group, a place, or a situation. In belonging, we square our edges into the whole, and we will fit, even imperfectly.

On Faith

Today the Google Doodle celebrates the Canadian athlete and cancer-research advocate Terry Fox and his Marathon of Hope, which happened when I was a child. I followed him by way of the nightly news. Images of Terry Fox running with his loping gait and bobbing curls, his face sometimes set grimly, electrified me as a young girl who had competed in her very first track meet that spring. Starting in Newfoundland in April 1980 and running on a prosthesis due to a leg lost to cancer, Terry Fox ran 5,373 kilometers across my childhood home of Canada. Terry covered at least a marathon's distance a day, until his effort was cut short by a return of the cancer. However, he succeeded in raising his goal of one dollar for every man, woman, and child in the country at the time, or $24 million, for cancer research. He stated, "Anything's possible if you try" and, of his audacious objective, "I want to try the impossible to show it can be done." We now take running and other sporting events completed for charity for granted, but doing so was unheard of at the time. Terry operated, literally, in uncharted territory, barely on the map, which is perhaps why he decided to run across the second-largest country in the world.

Terry Fox is among my heroes because he is a person of faith. I don't know whether he called it a Marathon of Hope because he realistically hoped for a cure for himself, but I am certain he acted from faith. He had faith in his ability to achieve something monumental. He had faith in his preparation and in his support team, including his parents. He had faith people would respond. And he had faith in our collective ability to find a cure for cancer, whether he benefited from it or not.

Perhaps the story of Terry Fox resonates so much for me because I am a person of faith. Faith has been my touchstone since I was a child. I have faith that there is a guiding set of principles available to order life, our understanding of it, our roles in it, and our relationships to each other. I find I act with integrity when I act in and through faith in those principles. Faith continues to be animating for me and to be at the root of my actions and decisions. Reflecting on it, I may be a person of faith because growing up I lacked security. Faith worked its way in to fill that gap. I found a form of security that I needed by investing in the principles of my faith; I could be certain of those principles because they became trustworthy through my practice of them.

Faith means a complete trust or confidence in something or someone. To have faith is to have a belief of trust. Faith is often conflated with religious conviction, such as a strong belief in God or the doctrines of religion, usually on the assumption that this is based on spiritual favor rather than proof. And certainly, those who cleave to religion often have faith in that religion and its doctrines.

But faith can relate to any strongly held belief or theory. To operate, faith must be solid, reliable, and strong. Faith can be unshakeable and unbreakable, particularly when it is evidence-based and arises from experiences outside you or from external events.

Faith is not popular in today's culture. Instead, we are a culture of skeptical ironists marinated in nihilism, and we have a culture fallen into hope. Faith and hope are not the same. Hope is a feeling; it is aspirational and full of expectation. Hope is a desire for a certain thing to happen. As a verb, hope can mean wanting something to happen or to be the case, or intending, if possible, to do something.

Carrying aspects of optimism within its meaning, hope launches from aspiration and ambition, brimming with wishes and desire. In this way, hope can be ephemera. There is nothing about hope that needs to be connected to the object of desire; there is no responsibility to connect hope to action. Hope is always separate from its objective; it references only an internal state. I am coming to understand the position of hope as a privilege. Hope develops staying power in momentum or inertia rather than from trust. Hope rarely survives a change in conditions.

Faith, on the other hand, takes knowledge, consent, and commitment. Faith requires choice and dedication. In Christian theosophy, this has been formalized in the three components of faith: knowledge, assent, and trust, with trust as the cornerstone. To have full faith is not merely to know something and to believe it, but to decide to act in accordance with that belief even when the conditions for success or realization are not always obvious or evident.

Only in acting on belief is trust made manifest, and trust must always be acted on, because trust can never be passive. Trust is demonstrated consistently by renewal. Trust is a continuum and not a point in time, which is why we speak about "breaking trust." Breaking trust is a rift in the temporal continuity of faith.

I have not always trusted in the elements of my faith, and it is during those breaks with trust that I have been at my most uncertain and bereft, or when I have acted contrary to my personal interests or integrity. I find fear continues to get the better of me. Fear, for me, becomes the break between knowledge and consent, or consent and commitment. Writing is an article of faith for me, and I might know that it is good for me and consent to that understanding, but I might stop writing, or fail to write something down out of a lack of commitment. Similarly, running is an article of faith for me. I know its beneficial effects on my body, mind, and spirit, but the breakdown often comes through commitment. Sometimes it takes work to run, and I don't run if I get lazy or afraid.

Courage, then, is essential to the expression of faith. And it is courage, too, or the introduction of courage to an aspirational situation, that can take one from merely hoping into the action of commitment required of and by faith.

For me, the temporal and physical dislocations of this pandemic period have tested my faith; without the ability to follow my usual routines, I've had to reflect deeply on how to spend my time and how to achieve in my days the practice of things to which I want to commit and recommit. I've reflected on how to move beyond acknowledging that these practices are important to me, and how to take steps to implement these back into my life. I've sometimes had to dig deep to act without fear during this period of uncertainty and anxiety, to bring these principles to the forefront of my life, despite all the changes.

It's a helpful reminder that acting with integrity is now and always the sole project and purpose of life. It's how you acquire knowledge of what's important to you and what you consent to doing with your time, talents, and intentions, and then to act with courage and commitment to bring those things to being, and to trust in them. That they are enough. That in them, and in the practice of faith, there is grace.

So today, I delight in and find solace in the Google Doodle and its celebration of the courage and vision that is the legacy of Terry Fox, shaped in part by his mother (who had so much faith and trust in him).

I see the Terry Fox story not as one of hope but of something far greater. Terry moved beyond hope into action, logging marathon after marathon in cold and rain, and likely in conditions that placed him in agony. Nevertheless, he persisted. He trusted, and he committed. And his example of faith and trust, and his legacy of action, gives us something solid to believe in, something tangible we can trust and act on. Faith is inherently generative and renewable. Perhaps that is why, forty years later, we continue to have Terry Fox runs in his honor.

On Exhaustion

I am exhausted. All week I've struggled to wake up, focus on tasks, and control my irritability. Yet this week I've also struggled to go to sleep and have often stayed awake beyond the hour I usually go to bed. Then my alarm goes off in the morning, and I snooze it relentlessly. All week I've wanted to nap during the day, and I've found myself lacking focus. And after I've brought energy to situations and tasks, following a burst of getting stuff done, I've felt drained.

So I do the little I can by writing this week. Despite my exhaustion and fear that this small set of words is not enough, could not ever be enough, I keep my promise to myself. I had promised and committed to myself that I would write one essay a week, week after week, for a year, no matter what happened. This would be my gift to myself, the activity that would give me structure through this year of unending calamity.

I had factored in how doubt would gnaw at my confidence beyond the starting line for these essays, and I expected the overall exercise to weigh on me. I suspected my fear of the blank page would rise and claw at me, causing struggle from time to time. But I had not factored in exhaustion, an epic weariness that suppresses clarity of thought and purpose, and how that might impact my ability and desire to write. How that might alienate my efforts to stay true to this purpose.

Exhaustion is a draining out of energy, of using something up or being used up completely, a state of extreme physical or mental fatigue. Being largely confined to my home and generally wanting for structured regular exercise, I know that my sense of tiredness does not arise from physical fatigue—how I would welcome a long hike or bike ride, or an excessive workout at the gym! In my current situation, I experience mental fatigue. It's tiring to be vigilant and ever on alert, as I have been over the past few months.

There's an exhaustion, too, from living in fear. For months, there was the thunder of unfamiliar noises here in Manhattan: the endless cries of ambulances, the banging of drums and caws of trombones, the pop of fireworks, the chop of helicopters. And there were weeks of eerie silence throughout spring, in which birdcalls shattered the stillness. The air in New York City is usually electric, but now the overall charge in the air of the country feels a bit unhinged, possibly dangerous in the exploitability of the unknown.

If exhaustion is draining, the metaphorical antidote to it is recharging, becoming refilled. Routine can be restorative, but this week I've found that my current routine feels like a trap, not letting energy in. The activities I often use to recharge—running, walking, writing—are achieving the opposite. Even in the writing of this piece, I feel what little reserve of energy I have draining out.

And yet, despite all my protests, there was enough energy to get this done. Today, I just hold on to that promise I made to myself and complete this week's piece. I push past the uncertainty of this project, this question of *what next?*, this fear of things falling apart. This piece has no purpose except to be done, and thus to be. If it is, then I was. I am.

Everything is always uncertain, and perhaps just to acknowledge this exhaustion of now is the work to be done. And to remind myself, too, that tomorrow will bring another day.

On Starting Over

I've had the experience of starting over. Of moving to another country during midlife to rebuild. I've joked to some that I emigrated to my own country, which is funny only because it's true. When I moved to the United States, I wasn't truly an immigrant because I already had citizenship. In that distinction, mine is not a typical immigrant experience. But I was a citizen without direct experience of what it meant to live as an adult and autonomous person in the country of which I was a citizen. While I am immensely proud of and grateful for my Canadian roots, I had an unending itch to understand and live within my American heritage. So, at an age when most people were hunkering down in homes and careers to reap the benefits of their station and build material wealth, I uprooted, walked away from everything I had, and started over.

Let me tell you: it's been the best and most catastrophic thing I have done. Exhilarating, liberating, frustrating, isolating, exhausting. It's hard to move across a country; it's harder to move across a border. Particularly when you move to a place in which you know almost no one and know even less about the place you are moving to.

In uprooting to New York City, I've had to start over almost from scratch, building new friendships, professional and personal credibility, networks, credit, and habits. Rebuilding a life is truly a marathon and not a sprint. Even after six years, I feel the work is only partway complete. I worry, sometimes, that I don't have the runway to finish the job.

It's remarkable what doesn't translate across a border, what needs to be reestablished. Credit, for example. My credit record in Canada was worthless in the United States. Equifax couldn't even see my Canadian rating, and in any event, the scales and ratings are different. So, I had to apply for credit cards without a credit record and went through a period of having to rely exclusively on cash while that was worked out. Not having a credit card in the US is challenging because of what it denies you. Amazon, Uber, and similar services of the current app revolution don't work on cash.

I lived transiently for the first couple of months I was in the US. I was in temporary housing without a fixed address, without ID that reflected I lived in the US, and without a permanent US phone number. I was caught in a circular loop of not having an address to get ID and not having ID to secure permanent goods. I was fortunate to have been able to front months of rent to secure an apartment and end that cycle. I'm really not sure how other less-established migrants do it, except through moxie and hustle. The day I went to the Department of Motor Vehicles with apartment keys and a US cell phone in my pocket to get a piece of US identification was a happy day for me, maybe the only time I'll ever be happy going to a DMV.

Professional accreditation was another thing that didn't translate. Some jobs travel better than others because they are skills-based, and you can take the skills with you. But I'm a knowledge worker and a lawyer, and law is highly localized. Not only did my Canadian credentials have no relevance to New York, but they also were not recognized. Fifteen years into my legal career, I was hitting the books, learning US law, and studying for a two-day multiple-choice exam. I wrote it across two humid days in the front row of a large room in the Buffalo Niagara Convention Center. I was surrounded by freaking-out twentysomethings, and while I didn't have the same amount of energy as these young adults, I had the wherewithal to focus and get a full night's sleep before the exam. Wisdom and experience are good for something.

Similarly, I didn't have an extensive professional network when I got here, but I did have some connections. I was extremely fortunate to have help finding a job, and I was met with and situated by colleagues from my professional network. But there was a limit to what I could rely on them for, and not all of them were based in New York. It was often company that I was lacking or someone to explain the most basic things. Like: How do you register to vote? How do the municipal laws and taxes work? How do you choose your bodega? What does my dry cleaner's side-eye mean? And most critically for living in New York: What are you really communicating with your method and amount of tip?

Even armed with professional accreditation and a professional network, I didn't have US experience before I got here. It showed, and that was humbling. Despite years of valuable and relevant experience, it was deficient in this new context, and I found I was relearning things every day. Things I could do in my sleep in Canada, such as filing documents with the court, were done differently here, and I had no clue how to actually do them. I had to learn anew how to ask for things, how to negotiate, the rhythms of business. It was like being a student all over again, but with no room for error since I was now an executive.

Similarly, I lacked the familiarity and credibility of established personal connections. I did not have a history of trading favors here, and I didn't "know the judge" or the person across the table from me like I did in Canada. I didn't have any Greek connections—didn't even know having them would be so critical here—and didn't have a college football team I was rooting for. I've come to learn that in some contexts, being a cypher is helpful; without being able to be pegged for my school, class, or Greek cohort, I am more usually judged on my own merits. But for years I felt like a salmon swimming upstream—and still do today.

When I moved, I did not expect the loneliness. There were endless weeks where I had almost no meaningful social contact since I had no actual friends in the city in which I lived. I came to value the immense generosity of frontline workers in NYC, who often fill the gaps of community for so many. There's a friendliness to New Yorkers that can be accessed; it's a social good that is invaluable, and people here know it.

What did help me during my move and integration into my new city were habits and plans. Those things that grounded me in my previous life proved to be the key to opening up a new life. Running was among the first things that connected me to the city, as I immediately met another runner and spent time jogging across Manhattan with her, exploring the city. Over time, I discovered running groups; now these runners are the bedrock of my community, and I count many as true friends that I can rely on.

Writing, too, anchored me. When I first moved to the city and knew no one, I'd walk to the West Village or Chelsea on the weekend, find a café, and write. I found drop-in writers' groups, discovered the Moth readings, and eventually connected with other kindred spirits of the pen for writing sessions in Brooklyn or Midtown libraries. Eventually, I made the Rose Main Reading Room in the great public library my writing home. Each of those spots embed me deeper into this city, and I have extended my personal connections as I've localized more places in which to write.

All of these gains have come at a cost, and it's still unclear to me the price of them. The move was dislocating to my career and buildup of wealth, as well as just expensive to do. I have no meaningful plan for retirement. Moving has shattered some relationships (though I wonder if these would have dissolved anyway). I often feel like I'm reliving my late twenties, although I'm a couple decades beyond them.

I also often feel divided in my situation, not only because my life has been literally bifurcated, but also because I feel like I live in two worlds, a foot planted in each but being neither fully present in either. Early on I wondered frequently if I should go back, but I have realized that there's no going home again, because the place I left is not the place that continues to be. In many ways, although Toronto was home, I don't know it anymore. I continue to work through the emotional weight of this.

Still, not many people have either the desire or the ability to start over, and this is what I have done and am doing. It's hard but wonderful work. It makes me conscious of the resiliency I possess and that humans are capable of. It has made me conscious of systems of culture and what we take for granted. It has sharpened my attention to change and my appreciation of constancy. I'm glad I did it, and yet I work toward getting it done. Immense gratitude to everyone that has shaped this journey.

On What I Haven't Done

It is sometimes said the measure of character is not how a person handles wins, but losses, that a legacy lies in how a person rises to confront crises and is remembered after passing. Likely that is all true, but we are not all called upon to stand before such a measuring stick. Many people's lives are quieter. Which is why I believe that the only focus for the measure of character lies in the quotidian: how you spend your time every day is what makes you who you are.

Although I have always aspired to greatness and legacy in the abstract, I have had no specific calling for this. I have no specific direction in mind for how to achieve my purpose and greatness, whatever they are. Honestly, I don't know why I was put on this earth, and I'm not sure that figuring that out matters. I'm here. My life is a series of days that I fill up with micro-decisions. I despaired of not having an obvious purpose or larger plan for years as a teenager and young adult until it dawned on me that the business of life was exactly these micro-decisions. The only question is what to make of the opportunities presented by such tiny movements. Making and implementing these daily choices is the pathway to fulfillment, for they help focus attention on what is important to me. My shift into gratitude became possible when I started to approach the business of living with attentiveness and detail. It is uncannily difficult and fulfilling. It can also be, when I indulge it, a source of suffering.

My paternal grandfather mentioned toward the end of his life that the worst thing you could say about a person was that he didn't pay attention. He had a story about his one regret: he signed a neighborhood petition without thinking about it. A family with a young boy who acted out, clearly from physical and cognitive disability, had moved onto the block, and the boy was sweet but sometimes disruptive. The neighbors passed my grandfather a petition about this family, which he signed "in a moment of carelessness." The family moved. I am proud that my grandfather saw through and owned the pain he may have caused this family in upending their safety and community, even though he could not take his signature back. I want to live in a world where my neighbors think about the consequences of their actions and work through them, however imperfectly. I want to live in a world of hard attention.

I've been meditating on the fine line between inaction and regret. It is said that the worst regrets are things we didn't do, but I have come to believe that inaction is only a necessary but not sufficient condition in which regrets can root. My major regrets are indeed things I didn't do, but that list also includes things I certainly *did* do. I am coming to see that my regrets lie more in situations where I did not pay attention. I have several examples of situations in life where I didn't act—I showed restraint—and those are some of my proudest moments. Quiet moments—a harsh word swallowed or a pause granted—contribute to peace and harmony without disrupting my own integrity. All such moments, borne out of micro-movements, are usually actions that are the equivalent of left turns on unfamiliar roads.

And even so, I catalog a list of Things I Haven't Done that reveal aspects of my character. These are not regrets, but things I haven't done that have shaped my character as much or more than things I have done. These steps not taken are the left turns I've made that have brought me to where and who I am today. Often these decisions have made me a more timid, insular person than my aspiration for myself. Some may calcify as regrets. Some may reveal a spine I had not anticipated for myself.

For example, as a teenager I dreamed of riding a bike from Alaska to Argentina, along the Pacific coast roads that run down the American continents. I had actually pulled together a lot of research on how to do this. I had a vague idea, too, that I would have, I don't know...written a book about it? But when it came to taking action, I didn't. My family was in crisis at the time, and I was keen to get away, but at what cost? I came to see this proposed trip as indulgent, me throwing myself into situations from which I clearly would have required rescue, because many of the places I would have gone were embroiled in war. I now see the restraint I exercised here as revealing a sensible aspect of my character. Whatever my desires, I think through the consequences of my actions on others. But I can tell you: oh, how I had wanted to do this trip! Instead, I've traveled much of this part of the world using other methods and when it was more sensible to do so.

Also, I had this idea that I'd take pictures of things, mostly people or landscapes, and write stories about them. This was in the 1990s. I bought a camera that was too expensive and started this project haphazardly. I never followed through, mostly because I never made the effort of setting up a darkroom, and I wasn't sure in any event if a chapbook of people and their stories was the way to go. Fast-forward fifteen years, and there are many examples of other people doing the idea I kicked around for years, but using social media rather than a small magazine format. They have done it and I did not, although now there are better tools for such projects. I could have made the idea work with the resources available at the time, but the distribution reach of the internet and the ease of using social media tools to reduce the burden of formatting and presentation for publishing make the project easier today, and that may explain in part why I didn't act on my idea years ago but many others have now. The unrealized photo project has taught me about the relationship of ideas to the context of opportunity and to be humble about the concept of originality. Any bright idea I have is likely one another has had too. But I am also reminded that intentional action is paramount. There is no substitute for creating space in life to do the things that are meaningful, and space takes boundaries. I have not always created and enforced boundaries to protect what is precious to me.

Over the years I have had multiple other ideas for businesses and have not followed through with them. People around me have been perplexed by my inaction on my ideas, especially in situations when I have *literally* handed them a business plan and list of opportunities. My entrepreneurial ideas happen so frequently that I can only describe them as persistent left turns on roads that have become so familiar, I am now driving around in a circle. I am leaning into my proclivity to generate new ideas now and paying attention. My choices show I have taken the road that leads to the background; I avoid the klieg lights. I'm primarily an idea person, but I also take deliberate steps into the role of spectator. I undertake the role of witness, of gathering testimony, of validating documents and discovering what the record is, of sorting the signal from the noise. This is my way of creating clarity from chaos. When I die, I might not have achieved anything great, but I hope that those I leave behind see that I have helped bring a little clarity to situations and left a record of events and a blazed trail for those who follow.

Most of what I haven't done, the actions I've taken, and the choices I've made may be known only to me. But I see, too, that I have followed a consistent pattern in *not* doing things. In moments of crisis, I've been dramatic but avoided creating long-term tension. I have paid inordinate attention to details and the consequences of action. In so many cases, I've seen enough to leave what's well alone and taken my adieu, passing the torch to others.

Much of my life, I've had two dreams persistent enough to wonder whether they are omens or memories from a former life. In one, I am in a small boat on a clear and cold lake. This is the place I drown. An owl in a tree starts to open its wings as I sink under for the final time. I am lost in nothingness, a cipher. In the other, I am on a ridge, looking over forest and rocks across the horizon. I am taking measurements for a map that I am creating. I hold a treasure of waxed paper in a portfolio across my chest and back. Although people have been here for ages, I am the first to encode this knowledge in new technology. I am a cartographer, and I am the first to record this location using these tools. I am aware that everyone will see how I interpret this ridge, and they will come here again and again, in droves. No one will know who I was, who I am, but they will know me from the lines that I will draw. Those lines are me.

I move through dreams of sleep and wakefulness. I am driving to destinations unknown, making left turns, and trying to pay attention.

On Adjustment

Now it's fall, and I remember that last year on this day I had a brilliant run in Chicago, running my twenty-first marathon to nearly perfect execution on a perfect-weather day. It was a remarkable weekend, in which the two-hour barrier to the marathon was shattered, and a woman set a new world record at the distance. For me, it also represented a return to distance form, and my first well-executed marathon race in several years. I was looking to lever that delicious run into an exceptional year of running ahead, to culminate in the fiftieth anniversary of the New York City Marathon to be run in 2020.

None of that was to be, of course. This weekend I ambled through Riverside Park on an easy seven-mile run. It was a beautiful early fall day, and people were out in droves, so I was masked the entire run. I kept on having to stop to catch my breath and adjust the wires of the nose-bridge. I marveled at how the year had turned out, so different than my expectations.

Humans are remarkably resilient and adaptable, even if we often don't want to be, because change is hard, unsettling, and challenging. And most of us don't like challenge; we like comfort. We aspire to change more frequently than we actually do. Although the one constant in life is change, we often choose against it. In other words, we are not terribly good at going with the flow.

Most of us are creatures of constancy: we stick to our habits and routines. We can comfortably handle whatever is thrown our way if it comes only from the drop-down menu of items we've seen and handled before. We select the same item from the same menu and call it a preference. We wear similar things and call it a style. We listen to viewpoints similar to our own, associate with people like us, and mold the people, places, and things around us to remind us of who we are. We move through life confident that tomorrow will be like yesterday.

When things don't turn out like they usually do, we can experience bitterness and disappointment, or sometimes surprise. When outcomes and events lie outside normal expectations, we experience a discontinuity. Sometimes this is experienced as shock.

Shocks are unsettling. Shocks can have physiological and psychological effects. Medical shock generally arises from the body not getting enough oxygen. The onset can be significant illness or trauma but can also occur after the body experiences disequilibrium or injury. The shock is the body's protective mechanism. It is a sign that things are not okay. Medical attention is often necessary to bring the body back to harmony and health.

Psychological or emotional shocks are also discombobulating. Denial or disorientation can precede longer-term effects, such as flashbacks, anxiety, irritability, or difficulty concentrating. Emotional shocks can express as post-traumatic stress disorder and can have long-term impacts on the body.

We don't have a great word for societal shocks, like the one we are all undergoing right now. We remain mired in a pandemic, on a cusp of an election that could be unsettling. Some of us have lost jobs, including jobs in industries that may be permanently changed. Our supply chains are cut or impaired. Our social networks are frayed. School, work, shopping, travel, entertainment, dining—all our routines are maladjusted, and we are having to reinvent how we spend our time, how we interact, and how we communicate.

We are all adapting to shock: first all at once, and then continuously. We are exactly where we need to be: on this journey, imperfectly adapting. Making modifications. Making all we have suitable for a new use or purpose, becoming adjusted to these new conditions. We fade in and out of despondency or panic. We plan "staycations" or moments of self-care. For those of us now working or schooling from home, we buy a second monitor or a stand-up desk and change our living quarters around. We schedule FaceTime and Zoom dates. We attend remote weddings, a thing I had never before thought desirable (or possible). We wear our masks, and some of us get very creative with them, fashioning them out of colorful cloth, or wearing masks with animal faces or slogans or signs to represent our interests.

We adapt and adapt further. Some of us slow down. Some of us develop new habits. Some of us actually spend time on the phone with people we've always cared about but for whom we've never really carved out time. Some of us are lightly affected, more inconvenienced. I count myself among this group.

Some of us experience deeper shocks. Death and illness. Temporary then permanent job loss. A significant move or temporary relocation. Some of us have expertise in industries, like travel or fashion or the arts, and need to be reborn. Some of us, liberated from commuting or jobs we don't like, are reflecting deeply about the how and why of living. Others unmoored from churches or communities are released from that commitment or find themselves bending toward greater engagement.

All this shock also requires adjustment. The work is moving from adaptation to adjustment, which means to alter or move something, usually slightly, in order to achieve the desired fit, appearance, or result. We alter, calibrate, rearrange, jigger, twiddle, and tweak. This implies tinkering to get things to fit better. This can feel a lot like adaptation, but the purpose and outcome are different.

In insurance, adjustment is the assessment of loss or damage when settling a claim. There is an acknowledgment of the permanence of the impairment or change, and closure of accounts in doing this work. What has been lost cannot be recovered, but it can be claimed and accounted for, and equivalence can be restored. This adjustment delivers an accounting of what was while leaving open the *to be*. This can be restoration, returning to what was. It can also be release of that lost part and change into something new when what was lost cannot be restored. But adjustment can leave you clear about the loss, what it is, and what it meant with the ability to move into the new, unencumbered.

There is always risk of loss in living; time is the great un-doer of stability and stasis. But in change there is opportunity. This year, despite the heartbreak and trauma, I have stopped to smell the flowers and found peace and joy. And on my runs, too, which are no longer for speed and distance, I take in the city.

Musicians, hungry for money and practice, and humans, hungry for music, find each other in a city park on a Saturday afternoon. A dance class erupts on a public walkway. Children whoop, and people let loose. There is celebration in the middle of, and despite, sadness. A saxophone wails and the drums beat time. We adjust loss. We dance, and clap, and sing.

On Masks

Last night I walked through Manhattan without a mask for the first time in months. It wasn't a deliberate decision: I had left my apartment quickly to go for a walk and had been distracted because I had just had an intense conversation by text with a photographer about being seen, about looking, about what the subject of a photo takes and leaves behind. I was thinking about how images can reveal what people try to hide, whether it's in the eyes or the way of holding a head, and the role of portraiture in revealing and concealing the masks that people wear to present and represent themselves. My thoughts were reeling, and my eyes did not focus on what was dangling from the hook right in front of my door. I was restless after a day spent inside and just wanted to be out, at night, to create a small distance from my careening mind.

But once I arrived outside and realized my oversight, the decision not to turn back and to continue with my walk marked this as a departure from what has become habit. Habit can be a face we wear, and consciousness of its slippage can shift attention to what is revealed. What did my eyes show, if anything, in that moment of awareness? Who was I when I made that decision to carry on, maskless, with my walk?

My whole walk was a departure. I walked in Central Park, at night, with headphones on listening to music, without a mask, during a pandemic. Despite hiding in the dark, there I was, revealed by my choices. And as I walked the middle loop, I passed all kinds of others not wearing masks, themselves keeping their distance in the shadows of trees. Everyone there was deliberately flouting recommended safety guidelines while simultaneously observing them. We were there, exposed, at night, without being fully seen. What a mass of contradictions we were, me and my fellow unknowns, each in our cocoons. What were we looking for, there in the darkness, amid slivers of light?

In this pandemic, masks are literal. We want solid, reliable, medical-grade masks to protect us from a highly contagious virus that is airborne. Despite considerable contradictory information about mask wearing and how to select an appropriate mask, we understand that in the circumstances we find ourselves, masks probably help. And because they help, we want them.

About the middle of April 2020, I bought five blue medical-grade masks from a drugstore for $15. At the time I couldn't believe my fortune in being able to find any masks for sale at all, and even as I paid cash and took them with a gloved hand, I felt a bit guilty. I was acquiring the kind of masks that doctors and nurses wear and used while doing their jobs, and it was unclear whether my buying them was materially reducing the stockpile available. Because they help, we want them, so we also *need* them. In times of scarcity, our attention focuses on need, which sharpens the distinction between needs and wants. We usually can mask the distinction if we are fortunate.

Now we are well past the stage of hoarding masks or feeling guilty that we are taking from frontline medical staff. Masks are now plentiful, both in a capacity and choice unimaginable six months ago. Styles and personalization abound. We can all choose the mask we wear and can make different choices from day to day. We can buy any mask we want, and many of us have more than we need. Masks can reflect personalities, political affiliations, tastes, and sensibilities. We can choose how to reveal ourselves from behind these coverings or even in our choice of whether to wear one at all. Who are we when we make these choices of whether or not to conceal, and under what kind of mask?

I am reminded of visiting Shanghai in 2018. Shanghai, I learned, is one of those cities in which the weather is expressed as much by air quality as temperature and precipitation, and this information is included in weather reports. In that gigantic city, masks are a health necessity. The population has embraced this fact, possibly with resignation. As I moved along the suburban streets of the neighborhood in which I was staying and into the underground train to head to the tourist area of the Bund, I noted the number of masks being worn and delighted in the choices people made: matching their masks to their outfits or reflecting a sports team, a video game, or some other passion. Or they just wore a boring blue mask, present and unremarkable. All throughout Shanghai, masks were prevalent and often personal.

Sitting in the downtown tourist area, watching everyone go about their business, I tried to pick out individual faces from behind masks, to see passing strangers for who they were. I discovered that masks reveal as much as they hide: the shape of a face is framed by how it is bifurcated; eyes are highlighted; hairstyles stand out. These Shanghai strangers filed past me for hours as I wandered about the city. I could see them, but could they see me? As a white woman alone in Shanghai, I was utterly different among them, invisibly revealed. I was sure they knew I was there by the way their eyes avoided me directly yet hit me from behind, but were they really seeing me? Were they able to take in the shape of my face? See my eyes? Remember my hairstyle? Could they see me? Can we, can anyone, ever really see strangers?

What a contrast, I thought as I walked last night past others whose faces also were bare. Many of their faces were empty, revealing little about what they were thinking. And in any event, we were all mostly concealed in shadow. Who were these fellow neighbors that I could not see but felt a kinship with?

Thinking about our literal masks gets me thinking about our metaphorical ones: the ones we put on daily for our friends and for strangers. The masks we choose in how we wear our faces and carry ourselves. How we experience ourselves in the world, and how we need and want to be experienced by others. How we use masks to project and to protect. How masks define us always, as much by what they conceal as what they reveal.

We cannot be known without being seen. We cannot know ourselves without the gaze of others. What we portray is never the whole of who we are, which encompasses the gap between what we show and what others see. While we pretend during this pandemic that we are wrestling with the novelty of literal physical masks, I realize that as a society we are also wrestling with the sudden awareness that we have been distracted by the illusion we have not been wearing masks at all. And yet it slips. Others are looking at us, and we are looking at ourselves. Will we let ourselves be seen in these new masks? Will they cover up or reveal what we had been wearing before? Are these old masks what we wanted or what we needed? And needed for what?

On Courage

Our culture fetishizes an idealized courage. In America, courage is big, and it is often strong and muscular. Courage is frequently depicted as physical power, or the capacity to resist attack, or the ability to handle extreme stress.

Popular culture often depicts courage in action-hero mode. In this vein, the elaboration of courage becomes associated with peak strength and, usually, with big weapons. We celebrate the courage of military personnel and first responders, such as police or firefighters, for specific actions: meeting enemy fire, capturing warlords, taking down criminals, suppressing riots, battling fires. We send battalions of actors into fictional battles against monsters, and we celebrate their courage dispatching zombies in performative blood-soaked orgies of gore. These images of courage have become particularly prevalent during America's unending war.

An alternative trope for courage is the human-interest story of overcoming extreme odds, frequently typecast as a battle with cancer or a debilitating injury. We call to mind the image of the solider with the prosthetic leg, the child gamely attempting to attend school in a motorized scooter, or the bald woman undergoing chemotherapy and radiation. These images showcase courage only as an act of facing the extreme often when the odds are long and tend to link courage with physical and psychological strength, which can lead to the unfortunate consequence of obscuring what may be most brave and courageous in these situations.

Bravery and courage are often conflated, but they are not the same. Courage is being afraid and acting anyway. Even tiny gestures can be courageous when these take a person past fear. Fear is an emotion induced by a perceived danger or threat that causes physiological and behavioral changes, such as fleeing, hiding, or freezing. Fear can occur in response to current or immediately present stimuli or in anticipation of a future threat perceived as a risk. Courage therefore involves acknowledging and managing one's emotional response then acting.

An act of courage frequently exhibits bravery. Bravery is the quality or state of having shown mental or moral strength to face danger, fear, or difficulty. Bravery can be more capacious than situations that involve fear because difficult situations may not involve confronting fear. Bravery may also involve confronting ethical and moral complexity. Often, one is exhibiting bravery when one confronts indifference, anger, depression, or anxiety. Bravery requires acknowledging and managing any one of a variety of negative emotions and still acting.

Exemplifying either courage or bravery is not an act of physical strength but an act of love: of heart strength manifested through the discipline of managing emotions, usually fear and the anger that sits on top of fear.

Demonstrating courage and acting with bravery is to aspire to and become involved in delivering justice.

We are instinctively called to celebrate courage when it manifests the character trait of bravery. Soldiers and first responders can be brave and often are when implementing discipline and restraint through proportionate action against the vulnerable in chaotic situations. The soldier receiving a prosthetic may have acted courageously in battle and also demonstrates bravery in persevering with rehabilitation, despite pain and frustration. The patient with terminal cancer is brave when she battles internal emotions and recommits to living each available day to the fullest, with love for herself and those around her. A child growing up with disability exhibits bravery in learning to live in a world that excludes him, leaves him behind, and does not accommodate him.

Often bravery is called for not only in the extreme circumstances of long odds but also in those situations that are most unjust and the least necessary, proportionate, or fair. Bravery is the stuff of the everyday, but we obscure how it threads through our lives by showcasing courage as the act of larger-than-life heroes. Turning courage into a superpower makes it seem out of reach and devalues its role in our own lives. If we only see courageous action as the purview of a select few, experienced only in extremes, do we discourage accountability in all of us for being brave?

Any person may demonstrate bravery and courage in countless ways every day. Courage lies in curiosity about the world and other people. It can simply show up in trying something new and risking failure. Acknowledging that you need to change and grow involves courage when the challenge is fear of what comes next. Letting go of a situation or a set of behaviors or beliefs that no longer serve you shows bravery. Courage is reaching across the aisle in the dispute, trying to make peace or find a middle ground although you fear rejection. Reaching out to someone in need can be an act of bravery. Living and loving fully demonstrates bravery. Persevering when times are tough, seeking a more harmonious way, rectifying injustice—all of these acts demonstrate bravery and courage.

Retrenchment into one's position is not an act of strength, nor is it an act of courage. Physical strength and beating an adversary into submission do not require courage. Picking on the weak, infirm, and vulnerable is not brave. Failing to remediate wrongs and taking things for granted are not brave postures. And, most importantly, controlling your life into such comfort that you feel no fear is not brave, because courage comes from reasonably confronting fear and acting anyway.

I find it peculiar that ours is a culture that so venerates courage when we do not have the individual or group strength necessary to face unwanted emotions. I believe we need people to be brave and manifest bravery in acts of character rather than just celebrating acts of physical courage. Facing difficult emotions often reveals who we are, and what we believe in, stand for, and will tolerate.

I have two tapestries hanging in my living room that for me exemplify courage. They both have yellow tones, and I think this is perfect; for me, yellow has become the color of bravery, not cowardice. The first tapestry was given to me by an early love and depicts a butterfly opening its wings. It is my reminder that personal, emotional, and psychological transformation requires the courage to confront negative and difficult emotions, particularly anger and self-doubt. The second was given to me by my grandfather. Apparently, his brother received it from a local woman the day that US Marines landed in Japan after that country sued for peace in the Second World War. I am told my great-uncle was there to secure Tokyo, maintain order, and prevent looting. He fulfilled that mission and protected people who the day before had been his enemies. What did that woman feel, approaching this soldier? It may have been her way of suing for peace for her and her community. I don't know, but I believe she was brave.

Converting an enemy into an ally, whether literally or metaphorically, by turning one's demons into wings—isn't that the most brave and courageous thing any of us could do?

On Perseverance

In the depths of the pandemic, feeling a bit blue due to isolation and inactivity, I renewed my vows of daily practice. Performing this practice has made all the difference to my well-being and contributes to my perseverance during this time.

Since early adolescence, I've had a practice that consists of a bit of journaling, a series of push-ups and sit-ups, a meditative moment or three of breathing, and planning for the day ahead by writing a to-do list. I have not always been successful at implementing it every day, particularly when a busy job had me traveling. Over the years, I have sometimes fallen off my routine. But the first Saturday in April 2020, when I woke up to the shocking news that a mass grave was being dug not three miles as the crow flies from me, I realized I would come undone emotionally if I didn't bundle routine into my days. I was also battling a running injury at the time and knew miles of pavement and distance were not available as psychic salves.

I started slowly with meditation. Being unable to quiet my mind for the incessant ambulance sirens during the worst days of New York City's pandemic, I chose to pull a tarot card from the deck every morning and meditate on its dominant imagery. Soon, I returned to journaling about thoughts that emerged and recording what was happening around me. One journal turned into a second journal, and by June, I had run through every card in the tarot deck. I shuffled the deck and started all over. By July, I decided I'd add push-ups and sit-ups back into my daily routine.

I've just completed my ninety-ninth day of daily routine. Tomorrow will be my hundredth. And, with the strength emerging from my daily calisthenics, I'm back to running again, and I have set my first monthly distance goal since the pandemic began. In other words, I've structured a purpose around these small practices, and even though they take me only thirty minutes, I've found consolation, commitment, and clarity in completing these daily activities.

Navigating this pandemic is an act of endurance, and endurance requires perseverance. We are all tired, and it is easy to want to avoid wearing masks, or want to see others without distance, or get frustrated with public officials and each other. When tired, we can forget that many continue to serve on the front lines and don't have the luxury of frustration. When tired, we can turn inward and think of our own needs rather than the needs of others.

I'm a marathoner; I practice an endurance sport, and 26.2 miles of distance teaches one a thing or two about navigating the long haul. The motto of my first marathon coach was "The mind leads the body." When undertaking any activity requiring endurance, it's important to remember this: where goes the mind, there goes the body. Preparation only takes one so far; during a marathon race, having a mental game and applying focus, determination, and breaking things down into smaller bits are keys for me. When I got tired, thinking I couldn't finish the race, I would remind myself: *Just run the mile you're in.* I would promise myself that I would figure each mile out, one mile at a time. After all, a marathon is just twenty-six consecutive one-mile races, with no stopping between them. By breaking them down this way, I've run over twenty of them.

The reason for failure in most cases is lack of perseverance. Perseverance is achieved through persistence in a course of action, a purpose, or a state, particularly in the face of difficulties, obstacles, or discouragement. Persistence is sticking with something, continuing or repeating a behavior, and is often associated with practice. Perseverance also has a theological aspect, and it means to continue in a state of grace until the end, leading to eternal salvation.

Whether or not one practices or adheres to a religion, I've found that this theological spin has something to teach me. Only perseverance through persistence leads one outside oneself and one's immediate conditions, even in the most painful and difficult situations. Whether or not one intends persistence to lead to theological salvation, persistence is necessary to achieve endurance. As the virus teaches us, anyone and anything can endure with a little persistence. We, too, need to apply persistence in service of something larger, not necessarily only in returning to normal, but in achieving a state of grace that comes from having endured something difficult, and having implemented the persistent practice necessary to emerge stronger from it.

So I'll persevere: as the days shorten and this virus persists, I'm going to log miles, do sit-ups and push-ups, exhale breaths, meditate, and journal. And when that gets difficult, I'm going to break it down and get through each day, one at a time, focusing on my daily practice. I know I can endure and do this long haul.

Because I persisted.

On Marriage

This weekend marks the fiftieth anniversary since my parents' wedding. My parents were married on November 20, 1970, and had their reception at Hart House in Toronto. I have no pictures of their wedding ceremony, and there were no pictures of their marriage day hanging up in our house while I was growing up. But the photographs that I do have now tell a story, and this wedding seemed like a happy occasion. There's a picture of my mother in her bridal pantsuit together with my father and his mother. There's a picture of my parents as they slice their wedding cake. My father's parents are at this wedding, having traveled from Buffalo. My mother's friend Sheila sits beside her. My parents threw a party of celebration for their relationship, and people showed up.

My parents are celebrating their milestone over the weekend despite the challenges of doing so during a pandemic. Of course, my parents may think they are celebrating their marriage, as they put it to me, rather than their wedding, as I've noted. In the shadow of their milestone, I have been reflecting on the distinction and on whether and why it matters.

My parents separated on or before my ninth birthday, and my father left the house shortly thereafter. They remained separated for at least fifteen years before finally divorcing. Although they had lived together for a short time before they were wed, at this weekend's milestone they'll have been living apart for almost four times the length of time they lived together. In the fifty years since their wedding, they've been divorced for about twenty-five of those years and separated for about forty.

Those numbers say something about quantity, but only hint at the qualitative aspect of their relationship as I remember it from my childhood. I recall the acrimony of their separation and the time spent in waiting rooms of legal aid clinics. I recall their arguments, usually about money, but also about each other. I recall the screaming and, periodically, the sound of porcelain breaking against a solid object. My father moved into the basement, and my mother started speaking about him in the past tense. I remember, after I learned my father was gone, almost experiencing a sense of relief.

My father moved into another apartment and got girlfriends whom I took no interest in. My mother didn't or couldn't find another relationship. We—my brother and I—stayed with her. Even after my father left the house, the toxicity remained. My mother had little positive to say about my father, and I was left to believe that one stray word from me to him would have our child support payments cut off. I see now this was a form of parental alienation. But the impact of this belief was real: had you asked me, I would have said my parents viscerally hated each other and wanted to have nothing to do with each other.

In our little nuclear family, there is no shared sense of community. There was very little family before my parents separated and none after that. There are no shared holidays and no family traditions to upkeep. As soon as I was old enough to have a job, I always volunteered to work every holiday. Getting paid to be out of the house was far better than having to choose which parent to spend the day with. *Neither* was a meaningful option.

Children learn from their parents, and what I learned about relationships and marriage was this: it's fraught, or can be. Seeing a relationship break down up close when I was old enough to understand what was happening but was still too young to impact the outcome showed me the difference between a relationship and a marriage. The relationship is the foundation. The marriage is the house. You have to decide to build a house on a foundation. Maintaining the house takes work and a shared sense of how the additions will fit and what the decorations should look like. A house placed on a poor foundation is likely to crumble.

That much I learned early. But what I didn't understand in the case of my parents was what made the foundation shaky. My parents are both very odd ducks, and to some extent, each is possessed of a demon. I had always assumed that they had each been their own limiting factor in the marriage. That although these broken souls had found each other, neither had the skills to make it work.

Understanding the challenge of a marriage, I never evolved a rosy view of the institution. I never dreamed of a wedding, and in my honest moments, I would acknowledge that I have organized my affairs specifically to avoid such an outcome. When I choose to be witty, I'll remark, "Relationship, wedding, marriage, you get only two out of three, so choose well!" That's a cynical joke but one borne from my own experience. *You don't get it all* is what I learned from watching my parents, and I've often thought it's best to give the wedding away. The relationship is for the individual within the pair, the marriage is for the couple or family as a unit, and the wedding is for the community. My parents, as my thinking went, had taken the wedding, avoided the marriage, and went asunder feeding their own needs within the relationship. So much for "until death do us part."

Imagine my surprise to have my father tell me, some thirty years after their separation and fifteen years after their divorce, that my parents were frequently getting together in person to down bottles of white wine and catch up. Upon learning this, I nearly fainted.

Turns out they are friends, if not the best of friends. They gather on holidays, including their children's birthdays, to celebrate. They have email correspondences and phone calls. They seem to tell each other everything or almost everything. In speaking about my mother a couple years ago, my father confessed to still having a breathless crush and to getting woozy at the sound of my mother's voice. Whatever has happened between them in the past, time has mostly erased it. It's proof that relationships change and evolve over time and can be repaired where damaged, bringing both people a little closer to wholeness.

My parents married relatively late in life, and now fifty years on they are no longer young. Yet they remain together, perhaps now more so than ever. I hope this connection brings them joy and continues to for years to come. I am baffled by it, but I recognize that whatever they have going on is theirs and theirs alone. Although my brother and I are products of their relationship, it is not about us and not for us. They have their thing, whatever it is. I choose to see this as positive and as some sign of redemption or hope—if not for them specifically, then perhaps generally for all of us. For me, too, their relationship has been healing. I've had to put aside the past and loosen all anger over what transpired when I was a child and how it impacted me. If my parents choose not to hold on to the past, why should I?

Fifty years after their first celebratory party, tonight we're having another one, our little family on a Zoom call. They are throwing a party of celebration, and my brother and I are showing up. Although their marriage didn't work, they've taught me something deeper about relationships, and their enormous value over time in healing what's broken.

Happy anniversary, Mom and Dad.

On Teaching

If a way to understand a person is through what they do, then I'm a teacher, even if I don't often describe myself that way. Over the past twenty-five years, in every year but for three, I've taught in some capacity, always to adults, and frequently in a university. During my last year as a college student, I taught a single lecture on the T. S. Eliot poem "The Waste Land." I remember my nervousness lasting for what seemed like days, and then the electric moment when a hand went up and my interpretation of a line was questioned, then challenged. The dialogue that followed, as more students joined the conversation, got me hooked on teaching.

The two gaps I've had from teaching were during my first year of law school (when I was overwhelmed with learning myself) and my third and fourth years in New York, a period that had me itching to go back to the classroom. Then I was offered an amazing opportunity to develop a course at the graduate level at a law school, and the only guardrails were that it had to be about law, technology, and innovation. I started with a blank sheet of paper and developed the course I always wished I could have taken, a course I jokingly refer to as "Law Behaving Badly." We look at what happens when technological development moves faster than law and draw instruction from social media (endless content), online bullying and harassment, wearables and bioethical hacking, contracts for smart devices, and augmented reality. At first the school was apprehensive about the curriculum, but it eventually gave me the green light. Despite my work schedule, I've somehow managed to keep teaching that course. Yesterday I finished teaching the fourth iteration of it.

I love teaching; the process of it gives me a thrill. I teach through discussion, and I'm awed at how much I learn each year from the students. Teaching for me is a mechanism of discovery; even when I think I know something, I can find new ways to look at the same questions and unfold deeper layers of understanding.

I get inspired watching people learn. Sometimes it seems as though I can see students handling the ideas as they rummage about and unpack the readings. It's satisfying to watch people bump up against something new, try something on, and leave with it. Perhaps this is how a matchmaker feels once they create the conditions in which people meet; for me it's intoxicating to launch ideas into a room of curious minds and step back to see what happens.

I'm convinced, selfishly, that no one benefits from my teaching more than me. Not only do I enjoy the thrill of watching others learn, but I'm also certain I accrue the greatest additive value from the discussion. After all, I'm the one who's chosen the topics and the readings, so I'm bound to find the subject matter interesting.

My long unfolding as a teacher stands in contrast to my history as a student. I'm ambivalent about so much "schooling," and I chafed and struggled against formal education even as I immersed myself in school. I knew from the youngest age that education was going to be my ticket to opportunity. I loved books and reading and learning. But I struggled with the prevailing teaching methods, and sometimes my grades in school came only with effort and at great personal cost. I could understand many abstract concepts easily and verbally express lots of information, but I struggled with math, which was taught by rote learning and memorization rather than problem-solving. I could be left to my own devices and learn unimpaired through reading, but I struggled to stay level with the other children during group work.

At the same time, I idolized many of my teachers. Teachers can leave an outsize impact on their charges, and that was certainly true in my case. I remember almost all of my elementary and secondary school teachers and librarians, and my high school teachers have had a lifelong impact on my personality and well-being. Among the precious gifts that a child can receive is the attention of an emotionally disciplined and judicious teacher.

As I got older, I began to understand that I'm a kinesthetic learner: I learn by doing after watching, and that learning style accounted for many of my challenges in elementary school—and why I did so well in hands-on classes like music, art, and shop. By the time I got to college, I could adapt my programs to subjects and teaching styles that worked well for me. Courses that allowed me to choose the paper topic (even unrelated to the reading list) or that permitted me to develop my own evaluation worked best for me. Paradoxically, arts gave me greater control over my evaluation forms and formats than science and math, which is why I ended up following a humanities path despite my natural inclination toward technology. Computing, in particular, always afforded me the greatest opportunities for hands-on engagement, but it was not taught in school when I was growing up.

But for now, my lecturing for this law school cohort is done. This part of the semester is a bit of an emotionally ambivalent time for me: I no longer get the thrill of seeing the students in person or even across a Zoom call, but I await the final papers with anticipation. Of course, now that I teach the course I wish I had taken, using evaluation methods I wanted for myself, I let the students choose any topic they want to write about. I won't even suggest one. I won't even hold them to producing papers, and I've received PowerPoints, graphs and databases, and strange combinations of deliverables. I'm grateful to the school for letting me gently push the boundaries of how and what I can encourage others to explore, and I am particularly grateful to any student who has spent any time in my class. Thank you, thank you, thank you.

On Impermanence

A broken coffee pot has me meditating on change and impermanence. After my French press shattered, seemingly over nothing, I was temporarily sad: I'd had this coffee pot since 1989, and it was one of the first adult things I'd bought. When it broke, I felt like I was losing something, almost like a part of me was disappearing. That coffee pot was among the very limited number of objects that I've portered around from place to place over the years. I've moved twenty-one times since I acquired it, so, bizarrely, this French press has been one of the most permanent and stable things in my life. And now that its replacement has arrived, I am reminded that everything is impermanent—except impermanence itself.

My French press was such a trusty stalwart. I reflect on its capacity, its capability, and how much of my time has been underwritten by this simple object. I can't even imagine how many cups of coffee and tea it has made over the years: Thousands? This device, over the years and one pot at a time, accomplished much, and I am humbled by how much we take our ordinary things for granted. I reflect, too, on how time accumulates and understand we can harness this temporal accumulation only if we are as patient as this coffee pot. It reminds me that effort and consistency are everything. Greatness can arise from a constellation of tiny gestures repeated with enough consistency to build a skill. For most of us, a legacy is not a thing that we do but a series of habits we practice. The impermanence of this object reminds me, above all, that things, like people, are designed for utility and service, and I must be uncompromising in determining my utility and service.

It is all too often the moments in between that are the stuff of life. What we did and the people who were there in all those ordinary moments are our bedrock and our mirrors, as much and perhaps even more so than who was there at the big moments. No doubt my French press fueled study sessions in high school and college, breakfast and brunch coffee binges, afternoon kaffeeklatsches, and late nights writing letters or legal briefs, underscoring the relationships and outputs by which my days have been constituted. Most recently, this simple French press has become my lifeline to coffee during the pandemic; the ritual of making coffee seems to be the one and only thing I can use to measure the passing of one day to the next. This coffee pot reminds me that I am defined by all of those pieces of time, and the people I was with, and not just the big events in my life. It is how we manage the flowing moments of time that compose the harmony and direction of our days.

This coffee pot has welcomed the world: frequently, beans from Indonesia and Nicaragua and Guatemala, beans from Hawaii after a glorious trip there in 2007, beans from a 2001 trip to Costa Rica, beans roasted in Italy whenever a neighbor in Toronto would bring them by. And it's helped me host people from around the world: Guatemalan refugees, with whom I would share coffee and explain how to get a bank account during resettlement; employees and collaborators; fellow students; and guests from Australia, Japan, France, South Korea, and Argentina. I realize how blessed I've been to see all those places and meet all those people. I realize how I've taken travel and my ability to meet people for granted. And I realize how long ago some of those visits were, how I've lost track of many of those people, how we've moved on, how people come and go and enter and leave our hearts. How all those impressions remain, however lightly, and how critical those impressions are for exercising and building the muscles of our hearts.

My French press gifted me coffee as I've read and expanded my mind, whether in formal schooling or in that period after schooling ends and real education begins. How many books, dogeared or borrowed, have I laid beside this coffee pot? Every Christmas for two decades, it's been by my side as I've started the day with a novel. Most recently, over Thanksgiving, I read a novel while cozied in flannel, with the French press and a cup of coffee beside me. I have already forgotten what I've read and realize I have forgotten most of what I've ever learned. At some point I knew the animal kingdom from a book, but now I couldn't define an amphibian if I needed to.

For years I carried so many things with me: books, clothes, photographs, furniture. I've moved from Toronto to Kingston to Montreal to Toronto, moved many places within Toronto, and then moved to New York. Time passed, and I accumulated. And when I moved to New York, I was confronted with all this stuff, much of which I had acquired thoughtlessly. Over the next five years, through an effort of will and another two moves, I winnowed my possessions down further. I realized I held on to things to remind me that the people and experiences I had when that stuff was present were real. My clinging resulted from a perception of loss: that people, things, and time were slipping away. And, of course, that's not right or helpful thinking: the only thing that is ever slipping away is time. Objects and people just come and go, sometimes passing through our lives where journeys intersect in space and time. Whether by randomness or chance is irrelevant: things and people aren't ours. They are impermanent, like us.

And then the French press shattered. Just like that, without so much as a bump against it, the glass carafe cracked. One day we, too, will have our moment where we crack or break or just stop ticking.

I've replaced my French press with a brand-new one. And I've also bought a milk frother so that I can make fancy drinks all by myself as the next pandemic wave hits. I'm grateful to my old pot for providing me with coffee for so many years, and for breaking and offering me this opportunity to reflect on all those years in this gentle way. And I'm excited, too, about what this new French press represents; as a cipher of change, it is a grounding in the present moment and an opportunity to renew thinking about impermanence.

On Disgust

This week I've experienced disgust twice: that sickening, visceral feeling of revulsion, an adverse reaction to something considered offensive, distasteful, or unpleasant. Disgust is an emotion and contains a range of states from mild dislike to intense revulsion and is triggered by the belief or feeling that something is repulsive or toxic. I experience it as a sudden, involuntary sense of alarm, and in my more intense feelings of it, I can experience a tightening of the stomach and a need to vomit.

The word is a variant of the medieval French *desgouster* and originates from the Latin *gustus*, or "taste." Disgust is often triggered by things that smell or taste bad, such as food that is "off," feces, or something rotten or decaying. But it can also be triggered by visuals, sounds, or even ideas.

In the latter sense, we can conflate disgust and disapproval, a feeling on the milder range of the emotional state of disgust. Someone can resign from a committee "disgusted" over the inefficiency of the meetings, or one can be "disgusted" by a bawdy joke. I used to think these usages of the word *disgust* were hyperbole and that the word should not be used for the milder states of disgust, such as dislike, aversion, distaste, and repugnance. I believe use of the word should be reserved only for those situations that triggered states of the greatest emotional intensity: revulsion, abhorrence, and loathing. While I'm less sure of that now, I do know we need to pay attention to disgust and how it metastasizes.

The disgust I experienced this week arose from the discovery, on consecutive mornings, of water bugs in my kitchen sink and bathtub. Now that I have dispatched them, I reflect on my emotional response and my reactions to discovering them.

I discovered the first one in my kitchen sink. It was large, about the length of my thumb, and had a shiny carapace. I was surprised and horrified, and had to swallow down shock and revulsion. It's really quite extraordinary what I threw at that insect. In addition to trying to drown it in the sink—an impossible task since the water pressure was not great and it was washed into a drain that it was too big to go down—I trapped it under a glass. At the suggestion of my landlord, I poured vinegar on it not once, but twice. This may have caused the insect to expire. The next day, I sprayed it with Raid, even though by then it was lying on its back, in the drain, with its little legs curled up against its body. Shortly after that, I discovered a second water bug in the bathtub, and again drowned it in vinegar and sprayed it with Raid.

I detail this catalog of my cruelty in part as a form of penance for the destruction of two creatures, but also because I consider myself to be a reasonable sort of person, and yet, confronted with disgust, I behaved like a maniac. I was simultaneously unable to kill the insects quickly with a squish and not able to tolerate them being alive in the same space as me. As a result, the drama of disgust played out in a protracted pantomime of suffering. A few months ago, I'd trapped another water bug under a glass in my bathroom, where it sat for over a week until a helpful friend came over and "dealt with it" for me. During that time, I had to step around the glass every time I went into my tiny bathroom, and I experienced nightmares about the bug getting out from under the glass and trying to engage me, Franz Kafka–style, in an analysis of my motives and behavior for imprisoning it.

This time, in another pandemic surge, I didn't have that "assist" option and had to address my loathing of the water bugs being alive in my apartment on my own. After I had chemically bombed them to death, I had the second revulsive reaction of having to deal with their carcasses, as in both cases I could not simply flush them away. It likely would have been hilarious to an outsider to see me crying and shaking as I tried to scoop the bugs up with a long-handled spoon and get them into the trash. Now that my personal crisis is over, I can see the episode as funny.

Disgust is an interesting emotion. I noticed, even as I experienced the shock of revulsion, that I was angry. I believe I was angry at experiencing the emotion of disgust so intensely. In my cognitive confusion, it was easy to transfer the emotion of anger to the source of my disgust and direct the anger at the water bugs. Disgust is an aversion and often motivates turning away or leaving, which is a sensible thing to do for toxic or polluted food or water. Anger, however, is different. Anger can draw one in and toward something and provoke violence. It may have been the anger, and the fear it engendered, that motivated my overreactions toward the water bugs.

Sometimes I see people call those they consider *Others*—such as refugees or migrants, the ill, the disabled, or whatever they might fear becoming—by the names of what may provoke disgust: cockroaches, vermin, or worse. Perhaps people call Others these things to convert pity to anger through the mechanism of disgust. We must pay attention when this is happening and how it impacts us. Disgust hijacks our higher reason. Disgust serves a critical function to keep us safe from toxins, but it can play havoc when we are not really at risk.

I'm not sure what to do about any of this, but I believe that empathy plays a large role in reducing the feeling of aversion and the response to this emotion. Feces is objectively disgusting, but parents learn to deal with it from their own children. Blood and bodily secretions can provoke disgust, but medical professionals manage these—and worse—on a daily basis. I am hopeful that we can unlearn disgust in the right contexts and when we are not really in danger. I have hope that I can learn to deal with water bugs in a saner, more measured way. And I remain hopeful that we as a society and a species can unlearn our fear of Others, and retrain that anger toward empathy, toward rushing in to help, not to condemn.

But I'm also realistic. I'm still disgusted by water bugs. My friend told me to buy traps to keep them away. I guess, today, I'll get some and set them out.

On Risk

Much of our linguistic map originates from locations so obscured by time and history that we often can't get our bearings and determine whether a word we use is a way station, a siding, or a transit to a future destination. So it is with the word *risk* and its complex emotional associations. "No risk, no reward!" evokes both hesitation and caution, as well as boldness and daring. Risk-takers can be fools who gambled everything and lost, but also heroes who persevered and achieved success despite danger or unlikely odds. Risk incites the passions of adventure and whispers promises of material security and love. No domain of human experience has avoided the pithiness of exhortations to risk. But in this, risk seems to cover every element of human experience: Can something be at once risky and also not risky? How do we determine risk? If risk is everywhere, how do we function?

We associate risk with the possibility of loss or injury. When an investment carries a risk, we understand that it could lose value. In the early days of insurance, when contracts protecting maritime expeditions and the potential of cargo were agreed to in the coffeehouses on wharfs, risk underwrote these ventures; the determination of risk in contracts of insurance was an early evolution of capital funding and cash management. As an insurer, you could underwrite a ship's successful voyage and reap the reward when it returned with valuable cargo. But the converse was true too. A ship could befall a range of hazards, both known and unknown. The ship, its crew, and its cargo could be lost, requiring you to pay out or forfeit your investment.

Thus, in insurance, the risk is the chance of a loss or a peril to the subject matter of a contract. Risk also denotes the thing that is a specified hazard to an insurer: the insurance hazard itself. In this sense, the word *risk* indicates the thing that creates or suggests the hazard, or the thing that brings about the potential of loss. Risk is *liminal*: it is the loss, as well as the chance of loss, as if the conjuring of the thing increases the likelihood of it happening. Risks and hazards travel together.

Hazard means a source of danger, be it an obstacle on a golf course or a material that requires special handling because it is noxious. But we describe events as originating from hazards too; for example, *hazarding a guess* means to take a guess, and this meaning implicates an archaic use of the word rooted in gambling. Hazard was a game of chance, played with two dice (from the French *hazard*), and so the word *hazard* also carries meanings associated with the effect of unpredictable and unanalyzable forces in determining events. In gambling, one's risk of loss is bound up in the roll of the dice, something over which the player has limited control. In undertaking the game of hazard, the players could win or lose money, seemingly at random.

Within this sense of the word, a hazard is a bad thing either that you couldn't foresee or that you could foresee but just couldn't tell whether it would impact you because it was unpredictable or uncertain. It's the chance or unpredictability that makes something a risk, not the underlying danger itself. Something can be very dangerous, but if we know how to handle it and have a plan for that danger, the risk will be reduced or eliminated. In other words, risk occurs because we don't know or can't know for certain. We reduce risk by diminishing the unknown about a hazard, not the underlying obstacle or danger itself.

Consequently—and it's easy to gloss this over—a key part of early insurance underwriting (literally, writing your name under the contract) involved investigation: learning about the captain and crew, the vessel, the voyage, and the plan, and trying to understand all that could go wrong. Critical to successful insurance is diligence: getting information. Information gathering is also a critical aspect of diligence in investments and is deemed necessary for pricing the risk.

When we risk, we are not heroes or losers, just people acting without full information, smoothing over the gap of knowledge, and acting anyway for better or worse. We act because we choose to, because we believe we have no other options, or simply because we determine that the option we choose is better than a competing one. Risk is a function of information.

Risk can be contrasted with trust. Trust is certainty; it is the opposite of chance. We often believe trust is an instinct or an emotion, but I don't think so. I believe trust is a calculation. We just might not understand trust to be a calculation in cases where we compute inputs in a split second. We can trust when we *know* something, when we have full, complete, and accurate information about it (or believe we have it).

Trust has both qualitative and quantitative aspects. What changes a risk decision into a trust decision is the trueness and the completeness of the information inputs, including emotional information. It's not only taking the time to evaluate the quality and reliability of the information going into the decision, but also slowing down to assess whether the quantity of information required is also available. Often a risk emerges because of something we didn't think of, but if we had thought of it, the information could have been available to us if we had looked for it.

Gamblers, for example, can adjust for risk by understanding the game, often by constructing detailed mental models of where the cards are, by resorting to statistics, or by using tells. They develop models based on information. Consequently, they can calibrate their bets or expenditures of cash to the circumstances. So, too, with the professional insurer or investor. It's no surprise that insurers and investment houses are among the most mathematical of businesses, employing quants and avoiding black swans—the unknown unknown—in order to diminish the hazard.

Risk, then, is an invitation not to adventure but to knowledge. To sense or to be present to risk is to become aware there may be things we don't know or understand. Risk is not to be feared, but to be broken down and embraced. We do not need to fear what we don't know, for these are just gaps in our knowledge. It is only the failure to fill in the gaps, either by not seeking out the right or enough information, that acting in the zone of risk increases the potential for hazards.

We wager big when we understand what's at stake—what we have to win and what we have to lose—but also when we understand how to calibrate our energies and resources, when we are able to take aim, and when we recognize when and where our adventure lands. We cannot live without risk and the attention it demands—it is the thing that makes life alive!

On Grace

Today my head and heart are full of grace. I have been pushed into this state, reluctantly at first and by degrees, until I felt as though I received it against my will.

As a culture, we trivialize grace by making it seem available without pain or reflection. We expect to receive grace from others unbidden but forget to, or do not, reflect on the consequences of that belief. Many of us worship grace as an image of beauty, particularly within the female form or as an artistic embellishment. We forget that grace can be sought but not demanded. Grace emerges within us from outside us, and its attainment is frequently a product of courage and faith exercised consistently.

Grace is unmerited divine assistance given to humans for their regeneration or sanctification, which is the act of making holy. In Christian theology, it is the act of God's grace by which the affections are purified and the soul is cleansed from sin and consecrated to God. But it is not necessary to be a Christian or to believe in a god or divine being to experience or be interested in sanctification. In a more general sense, the meaning of *sanctification* is "the state of proper functioning." A musical instrument is "sanctified" when it is used to make music. A pen is "sanctified" when it is used to write. In the theological sense, things are sanctified when they are used for the purpose God intends, and a human being is sanctified when he or she lives according to God's design and purpose. In a more general sense, any of us can become sanctified when we align with our proper functioning.

Grace can be a complicated aspect of Christian theology, but within that worldview, humans cannot sanctify themselves despite being called to do so even within the Bible. Several Christian traditions also maintain that no one can presume on God's grace in sanctification, and from this belief emerges the emphasis on good works, which are demonstrations of trust in, obeisance to, and devotion to God.

So, I am returned to contemplating grace. As it is unmerited divine assistance, we can seek it, but not demand it. The state of being sanctified means that we have accepted we must act with faith. Maintaining a state of faith may take courage, particularly when things the world throws at you seem inconsistent with grace, sanctification, and proper functioning. To be in a state of grace involves finding and maintaining your purpose even while things around you are going haywire.

The events of the past year have been unnervingly challenging and painful. Significant illness, political controversy, economic and social dislocation, and the threat of war have all occupied the public airwaves. Our oceans are warming, we are losing biodiversity, we are drowning in and being hammered by powerful storms, and significant chunks of the world are on fire. There may be more human migration now, as a result of war and economic and physical insecurity, than at any other time in human history. Millions upon millions of people remain impoverished and food- and water-insecure. Millions, too, are at risk of unnecessary death from a virus as health systems overload and collapse. The vaccines in development, production, and distribution are a bright light that remains a pinpoint at the end of a long tunnel.

It is easy and possible to despair, to get angry, or to get lazy. It is easy, in other words, to lack courage and faith. And I mean faith, not hope. Hope is the emotion; faith is the belief that drives action. I hope for a vaccine; I also have faith that humans working together, armed with scientific methods, can find a way, given time and resources. Faith requires lean-in engagement to discern what is productive and fruitful. I am not a scientist, and so faith requires from me only this: don't get COVID-19, and don't give COVID-19. In other words, I have to play my part, small as it might be.

Yet at times, this pandemic period is hard for me according to my situation and abilities. It is hard being alone pretty much constantly and without any other human contact for weeks on end. It is scary for me to consider what might happen if I, alone, got really sick. It is hard to be so vigilant and to think about whether a sortie out of my house is "really necessary." I have had to make choices, some of which I didn't like. I have had to pay attention, ensure I did not put anyone at danger, and respond to the needs of my community perhaps like never before. I've had to think about the world I want to live in and what I can do now to ensure the world I want will be there when this is all over. What causes do I really want to support?

Do I need to volunteer or donate? If I can't be physically present for other people, how can I still show up?

Faith, whether aimed at a religious outcome or not, is always expansive and always enlarges. My attention and vigilance force expansion out of myself and into—and for—others, even though it started as self-preservation. I didn't let myself give up or give in, because too much was at stake for me and others, including those I didn't know.

This, I learned, is the state when grace may enter: when you are pushed, by situations often terrible and unpleasant, to the edge of your experience and comfort zone and find relief in turning compassionate attention to others in generosity rather than in fear and blame. The divine may enter there, as we become vessels for something else, which is inevitably our highest and best use, whatever that is. Even when, in the middle of a pandemic, one's highest and best use is sitting indoors on one's caboose making calls to check in on people and actually really, *really* listening this time, or just staying out of the way and not putting anyone else in danger. Grace reminds each of us that, so often, it's not about you or what you do, but when and how you show up.

I can't know how long I'll continue to experience this state of grace, and none of us who may have received it do. But it's made me very grateful for the challenges that I have been facing over the past year and the opportunities for personal and spiritual growth they have generated. In my new state of grace, I'm less anxious, and I struggle less against the world. I'm more disciplined and discerning in my thinking. I'm writing and running more, both activities central to my well-being. These small changes, inconsequential to the world, are necessary to me and those around me. In the end, those around me are what I have and who I am, so how I show up for people may be the most important contribution I can make with my time on this planet.

As a society, we have experienced trauma, and we continue to experience it. This collective trauma has exposed the fissure points and rifts between and among us, thrown images of injustice and suffering into sharp relief, and catalyzed strong emotions. Will our strong emotions overwhelm us? Will they germinate into faith? As a society, can we find collective courage to look at our traumas to move past our own fears and hurts and into territory that challenges us and invites us to be brave? It may be here that grace for us all lies, in that location of potential regeneration and sanctification that arises unbidden, invited but unmerited.

Time is on our side because we are *here*. We can be present and faithful, obeisant to our best selves and highest callings. Grace is available if we have courage to receive it.

On Joy

We have retired to bed after a campfire. I have chosen not to use a tent, and my cot is set up at the edge of the firepit. Behind me in the darkness is the Australian outback. While the fire dies down and I lie on my back, the sky overhead fills with magnificent light as the stars, constellations, and Milky Way emerge. I am transfixed watching the sky and its millions of points of light for hours. Never have I been in such darkness and such light.

I stand underneath a canopy of trees and look up. Lianas drape over tall branches, and monkeys are overhead, staring down at me. The rain forest is a riot of sounds. Multicolored parrots and other birds flit between the trees. The sky is the purest blue. I am enveloped in a fragrant warmth, and I close my eyes and listen to this symphony of life.

The lake is bracing cold, as many Canadian lakes are in late May. We have run down to the shore from the cottage, whose light is framed within the emerging night. We've jumped into the water from the dock and now splash around, all giggling like maniacs, night-swimming. My skin is aware of every ripple of cold water; my senses are fully engaged.

In all these situations I felt joy—something awesome and translational, something memorable. These events above happened in 2009, 2001, and 1990, respectively, and years later I can still evoke those memories in vivid detail and recall the specific physical sensations I experienced. I cannot obtain this degree of recalled specificity with other situations even though I remember being happy, contented, and I may be able to remember some specific details about those happy times.

A dictionary will tell you that joy is *delight*: the emotion evoked by well-being, success, or good fortune or by the prospect of possessing what one desires. A dictionary also, rather unhelpfully, defines happiness as the state or quality of being happy, a state of well-being and contentment: joy. But in my experience, happiness and joy are not the same. Joy is a particular expression of happiness; it is specific, remains present, and is visceral.

Happiness and its variants are something we may not spend time thinking deeply about. We may not even have taken the time to define happiness with precision because most of us know it when we feel it and might relate to it within a range of positive feelings including joy, gratitude, contentment, and pride. But all of these are distinct emotions. When we say, "I want to be happy," what do we mean? Do we want to experience *all* of these emotions, or will any one of them do? What does "being happy" mean?

When people say they want happiness, if asked to provide specifics, many revert to things that give them pleasure: a fine meal, time with friends, or a new experience. We recognize that pleasure is an emotion because we can also sense it. But pleasures such as these are always fleeting; all of the above are moments of time to be enjoyed, but they will pass.

Happiness, in contrast, is not transient; it is a state of contentment arising from the experience of having all one's needs met, when one is satisfied and fulfilled. Happiness often has a psychic component as well as a physical one: it implies a relaxation and rest of agita and angst that can sometimes grip one during moments of pleasure. There is an element of ongoing fulfillment in the experience and expression of happiness.

Joy is something else. If I think about times when I have experienced joy rather than contentment, pleasure, or pride, it's this: I have experienced joy primarily in situations where I have been immersed. In this sense, I have experienced joy as a complete surrender to happiness. Joy can transport us to an emotional state distinct from happiness, even if the emotion of joy may be indistinguishable from experience of the conditions that give rise to it. States of joy are hard to conjure. They are rare and precious. They are, simply, gifts.

I had been diving off the south shore of Kauai twice a day for almost a week. I know the reef and sandy shoals. My buoyancy in the water is now instinctive; I've perfected my oxygen consumption and can now stay underwater for over an hour on a single tank. One by one, everyone in the dive group surfaces, and I remain underwater with the master diver. Large tropical turtles swim by. Then she comes to us, tentatively: a monk seal. She slowly swims right up to me, staring into my mask. She rolls over and continues to look at me. I roll over. Within a minute we are somersaulting around and across each other in a spontaneous underwater game of slow-motion 3D hopscotch. Bubbles rise to the surface: I am laughing so hard that it's expressed as near-constant exhalations from my regulator. She barks.

Underwater isn't forever for alive humans. I have to resurface. As I spend a few minutes in shallower water to recalibrate my nitrogen levels, the monk seal stays below me, floating on her back and looking up, as though she wanted to remain as immersed as I was in our game.

Two years later, I am hiking the Bruce Trail in Ontario with a friend. There is almost no wind. The forest is peacefully calm, although we expect rain later in the day. The forest is lush, and I delight in its fragrance and perfect stillness. My friend snaps a picture. It is a wonderful picture of me, a tiny figure in black surrounded by towering trees, walking away calmly from the camera along a trail. But I don't need to look at that picture to return there. I can close my eyes, tap into the joy of that memory, and feel the presence of those trees encircling me.

On Boundaries

We are nothing without boundaries. A boundary is a line, often imaginary, separating one thing from another. Boundaries divide, and in so dividing, they shape. Boundaries create distinctions, which paradoxically can bring into focus that which we need to see. In creating separation, boundaries can catalyze attention, including of who we are in relation to others. Boundaries are necessary for being, and they define who we are.

It is said that all interpersonal relationships benefit from boundaries to avoid disorders resulting in inappropriate need or abuse. We say that individuals must "create healthy boundaries" and teach children how to "have boundaries." Without those boundaries, people cannot distinguish their own needs and desires from those of others and may project their intentions onto other people or substitute another's thinking as their own. We think of abuse as an act, usually some form of violence either physical, sexual, or verbal; and these violative acts and actions are real. But abuse can also be understood as a degradation of integrity of the self, a condition of being upon which others predate or that we compound with unhealthy, unhelpful acts. Integrity of the self arises from boundaries and having the skills to create and understand oneself as distinct from others.

In this sense the very young, who continue to learn particularly through mimicry, are vulnerable to abuse because they do not yet have fully evolved boundaries. And mental illness can be understood as an inability to establish boundaries or the absence of coherent boundaries. I've observed that sometimes the severity of the experience of mental illness can be proportionate to the individual's community, and I've wondered whether we can understand mental illness as a community of one, because the hallmarks of what is described as mental illness often involve the conditions in which boundaries do not exist or lack integrity. This integrity goes two ways: the person establishing the boundary can lose track of where it is or what it is for, and those across the line either do not respect the boundary or do not know about it. Abuse and disorder often follow.

Boundaries are also foundational to physical and mental health. The skin is among our most important boundaries, and we become injured when it is permeated. Currently, we are all wrestling with a viral invader that permeates the boundaries of our cell membranes and hijacks our systems to replicate itself, potentially causing severe illness and death. Other diseases propagate by impairing the calibrations within our systems and messing with boundaries between bodily functions and systems (are you a healthy or nonhealthy cell in my body?), thereby causing disorder.

Humans are social animals, and groups of humans can be understood metaphorically as organisms. For integrity, groups of humans also create boundaries as a mechanism for self-definition. Such boundaries can follow the tropes of tribalism or take on other delimiters, including those that refer to other boundaries, whether geographical, political, or sociological. One can define oneself by reference to one's country, membership in a linguistic or cultural group, a set of habits or practices, or a love of a sports team or movie director; in all cases, one defines the self by that around which one has drawn a boundary.

An individual human can belong to many such groups, and because most of those imaginary lines are invisible (and fictional), they can overlap and be seamlessly crossed without complexity. But sometimes, these boundaries conflict: the dictates of boundaries between one group and another can sit in opposition or tension such that a single person cannot logically be a member of both. To reconcile this state, the individual human may need to engage in cognitive dissonance, telling itself it can belong to both groups at once, even though the boundaries of each conflict. Such thinking in a person is disordered, and metaphorically it can become a malignant cell within one or both groups.

To describe things in the world, humans create ideas to define, circumscribe, or link together what is separated by time and space. We create ideas to explain events and observations with unclear causation. Ideas function as intangible boundaries, and humans use language to separate one set of explanations from other potential explanations. The creation of ideas constructs a sense of order. All ideas serve as boundaries, and when we understand this, we can start to appreciate that some ideas contain integrity and coherence within themselves as a way of distinguishing things in the world, while others lack the same level of integrity because of the ways in which they separate and divide.

Without boundaries between ourselves and others, between our bodies and the world, and without clear ways of describing these boundaries, we are ourselves indistinct and prone to inappropriate need or abuse. Inappropriate need looks like clinging—to others, to groups, or to ideas that no longer serve us. Abuse looks like a lack of responsibility, incoherence, or violence to the self or others. In the same way that it is our basic function as humans to create healthy boundaries to develop meaningful relationships between ourselves and others, and between us and the physical world to keep our bodies safe, we must also create healthy boundaries in our ideas to separate those that serve us in ordering the world from those ideas that do not.

We have no control over external events, circumstances, or situations; we have control only over our own minds and our reactions to external events. We have to make choices in how to think about things and how to order, describe, and act upon our perceptions. Are we clear on our ideas? Do we have healthy boundaries for ideas, and do we monitor and enforce these? Have we checked to make sure our boundaries continue to make sense, and have integrity of purpose and form? The more we experience disorder on the outside, the more at risk we are for unhealthy boundaries. We must decide how much the boundaries that define us align with our integrity.

We are nothing without boundaries.

On Writer's Block

The blank page has gripped me for over a week, including this morning. I've gotten curious and I'm feeling into it: What's got me so paralyzed that I've been unable to write? And is this related to other times when I've been unable to move forward on my projects and plans? What is this all about?

For a full ten days, I've felt particularly exhausted, which has led to lethargy and overwhelm. There have been mornings I haven't wanted to get out of bed and days when my head wasn't into the activities on my to-do list. A sense of burden and weight has lingered, compounding the exhaustion, and I've found myself short-tempered. Loitering within my daily planner over the past two weeks are tasks that get moved forward, uncompleted, every day. A couple work-specific deliverables hang over me. I can't even fully engage in escapism such as movies or books because I cannot get organized, and because I feel anxiety trying to relax with so much unfinished business.

I know from experience that breakthroughs happen when I dissect tasks into little bits and accomplish any piece of the whole to generate momentum. I also know that sometimes I just take on too much, and when I feel that burden, I spend time editing to-do lists of what is truly necessary to yield benefit and movement.

My current state is likely a product of fatigue: of quarantine and the vigilance it entails, of the routine of the unending quotidian, of the blankness of the calendar with no community or travel events to look forward to. I am retreating a bit into isolation. Our circles and our ambits are growing smaller, tightening to encompass only what we can control. Within this pandemic we are all learning, and wrestling with, the limits of what we can control. This is clarifying and liberating, but also alarming. So much is not within what we thought to be our grasp! Sometimes I get paralyzed thinking about how many things could go wrong, but then I am a worrier by nature.

And, of course, during this pandemic it can feel like the world is shifting under our feet. The stories that we have been telling ourselves are clearly a wrapping that is coming undone. Our systems are unraveling, both slowly and all at once. There's an awareness we are standing in the spotlight of history, most of us statistics.

I've been unable to fully process it all emotionally. There have been so many moments where I can't pin down or explain what I am feeling. These unprocessed emotions linger and create an internal weather pattern of chaos that I experience as paralysis. I spend a lot of time lying down or walking as mechanisms to process, clear, and expunge the emotions, many of which are unfamiliar and unnameable. I've come to realize that I'm an emotional introvert: I like my feelings one at a time so I can sit with each one quietly and come to know it. When emotions come all at once in a social group, I experience them the same way I encounter a large crowd: I can handle it, but I find such a gathering exhausting. This period has been particularly tiring for my interior ecology.

Focusing my reflections on the writing of these essays, I'm fatigued by this project and the doing of it, yet energized by the momentum. But something about the larger context has shifted this activity for me, and for the first time I've felt it as work, as a duty to myself and others to continue to produce these weekly essays. I have sat for hours on end in front of a blank page with single words scribbled in front of me—Resolution, Ambivalence, Fear—the purported topics I am going to write about. And nothing comes, except a feeling of failure and with it, guilt.

It was the guilt that got my attention and roused my curiosity. What was going on there? Instead of writing, I just sat with that feeling this morning and got to know it. I discovered I was feeling guilty because I had somehow turned this writing exercise into a measure of my self-worth and was finding myself wanting, with production as the measure. That lens had reframed the whole exercise of these essays, converting an amusement to keep myself occupied during quarantine and connect with my community into something much darker and more weighted. Something I had started and valued simply for the activity and ritual was ossifying. Why was I doing that? And was that what I was doing any time I became paralyzed?

Writer's block is real. I know because I experience it so frequently. I have "wanted to be a writer" for most of my life, and that desire has been frustrated simply by not writing, usually from this paralysis, which I've then come to believe defines my abilities. I've also given myself over to every excuse as to why I don't write: I've been in school, working, or meeting with friends. But those excuses are all about how I organize my time, and I have control over how I spend my time. The small victory I've had this year is that I've now seized control and assigned segments of each week to the activity of writing. And yet this week I've had to wrestle with this question: But what if nothing comes? What if I spend the allocated block of time in front of a screen and I don't connect my brain with my fingers on the keys? What if I am not a writer because I have nothing worth saying?

My writer's block is my emotions, I've realized, particularly when emotions conflict within me, or when I'm unable to focus on one emotion or pull it out and resolve it. The block is not nothing to say; it's not having anything to *feel* in a conscious way through writing. My curiosity over writer's block this week has led me here: writing will flow when I get curious about emotions and what causes them to rise up and resolve. Blockages in processing emotions create blockages in action, which for me show up as blockages in writing or doing. Of course, emotions and writing both require flow. Blocks. Flow. It all makes sense, and in thinking this through I realize, too, that we've already encoded this unconscious knowing in linguistics and word choice.

I used to think the saying "The pen is mightier than the sword" meant that thoughts would outlive and out-muscle action. After the past two weeks, I see that saying differently now, as suggesting that there is more lasting power from actions that arise from processed emotions than actions arising from unprocessed emotions. When we act without thinking through our feelings, it can be powerful, but most often destructive, since when we act in passion it is often from anger or fear or some derivation of these emotions. But when we process our emotions and keep within their flow, which can include writing them down, actions unavailable in the haste of moving away from the discomfort of processing become apparent. We enlarge our options and our sphere of influence. Staying in the flow can be harder, but it enriches us mightily.

I'm glad my curiosity got the better of me this morning. I've felt into the emotional blockages that have possessed me these past few days, and in that flow, I've gained new insight in words. Truly, the processing of the pen is mightier than the blockages of the sword.

On Change

The idea of change attracts platitudes. We know, or believe we know, that change is constant. But we also know, or believe we know, that change is hard. So, apparently change is constantly all around us but also difficult to achieve.

But what is change, exactly? And what is the mechanism of change? How does a person or system attain the conditions to move into the different action or the different state that is or indicates the change? What are the steps that a person desiring change can take to bring it about?

Change is several related things: it is the act, process, or result of making different. It is also the passing of one condition to another. And in English, change also refers to something legally used as a mechanism of exchange that also has value. In all of these meanings, change indicates transformation, whether through exchange, mutation, revision, amendment, or alteration.

Any time there is an exchange, there is change; when another person and I exchange things, whether money or goods or ideas, we end up with something different. And because we are possessed by things as much as we possess them, we are transformed, even in a small way, by the things we carry, own, or mind.

So it is, too, with intangible things such as emotions or thoughts; they can change us, or be used to change us, as much as having something new or losing things transforms us. Changing one's mind by substituting one thought or idea for another or changing one's view by feeling a different emotion results in being a different person by virtue of having those different thoughts or feelings. To have something altered about one's thinking or feeling alters perception and how one shows up in the world.

But what brings about change? Why do we decide to take on a new thing, idea, or feeling? How does change happen?

Loss, or the prospect of loss, can be a catalyst for change. There are several prevalent tropes of loss as triggers for transformation; for example, "hitting rock bottom" is used to indicate changing lifestyle habits after an illness, significant upset, or injury. After a shock, the human organism adjusts in an effort to find equilibrium. We take on healthy eating after a heart attack; we give up an addictive substance after a near-death experience or a painful emotional loss. Or a series of little losses of friends, self-respect, health, or financial stability simply add up and become too great. There is an adjustment, and one state is substituted for another: sobriety for addiction, kindness for busyness and indifference, mindfulness in eating for inattention from overwhelm.

I've considered that at the root of much of this transformation is fear, either in being moved by fear or adjusting behavior to move past or avoid continuing to feel fear. Fear can overcome us in a way that can be motivating. What is interesting to me about fear is that while it is at once a primary experience of arousal that is almost automatic, it is also a secondary *liminal* experience that we often express as another emotional and physical state, such as anger or focus. Anger and focus are aspects of the fight-or-flight response.

Loss, or fear of loss, can motivate this kind of transformation in more subtle ways as well. We fear the loss of someone's affection and undertake personal changes such as losing weight or a makeover or spending more time with that person. We fear loss of social standing and adjust our behaviors. We fear loss of security or comfort in old age and start saving.

The subtlety of this kind of change is that it can be rooted in desire, a state of wanting to move toward something rather than wanting to move away in fear. Desire is an aspect of focus, and I wonder whether the intensity of desire has its origins in the same bodily system through which we experience fear. Creatures crave experiences of pleasure and release as much as they crave freedom from pain and want, and behaviors and thoughts can be aligned to seek out these feelings, experiences, and states. We can organize ourselves to want and to have more of these pleasures and implement behaviors—changes—to secure them.

This lens on change is transactional and suggests that change can be both automatic as well as willed. Change happens for control, whether out of conscious or unconscious necessity or awareness. The body can catalyze us into change for equilibrium and self-preservation, although these adjustments might have a very short-term effect.

Other changes, such as those that come from semiconscious or conscious intentions, might have a much longer-term impact.

We don't always have clarity when it comes to change. We both underestimate and overestimate how these adjustments and alterations will play out. A very small change, such as the start of a small savings regimen, can lead to big results over the long term because of compound interest. A small change to a dietary habit or exercise regime can lead to long-term health. Reading for fifteen minutes a day from diverse sources can lead to insights with unclear and uncertain downstream impacts. Removing pain, such as through hygiene habits or medical attention, can lead to greater ease of movement and improved personal interactions. We often don't understand the full future consequences of actions taken today, which is what makes some of those changes so powerful and why they can be so scary: we don't know what will be unleashed.

Which brings us back to fear and another of its attributes: freeze. Confronted with the uncertainty of the future, such as whether an adjustment or an exchange may actually result in less pain and more gain, it is easy to become paralyzed and not do anything. But freezing and inaction are the same as deciding to do nothing at all. Situations, feelings, and conditions are likely to remain constant.

So, I return to the insight that we can implement steps toward change primarily when we root action, transformation, and adjustment in what we can control now. To understand what we can control comes from clarity.

Change comes, then, not from willpower, but discernment about what's in one's inner state and what one has control over.

We can't control what other people think of us, but we can decide who we want to be in the world, and what that looks like, and what behaviors to take to demonstrate our vision of ourselves. We mostly have control over what we put in our bodies, and we can decide where our boundaries are with other people and things. We can choose what things we want to possess us and where we want to direct our attention; in other words, we can make choices about what is important to us, both in terms of how we spend our time and how we react to things. We can't control how other people treat us, but we can set boundaries and define how we react when they are crossed. We can control the energy we give to others who don't use our energy with integrity and respect. We can say *no* to the things, people, and situations that do not nourish us.

We can get caught in dramas of believing we need to make large-scale change, convinced that these dramas are necessary and desirable, but such beliefs may be rooted in fantasies of control and stability that exceed what is available. Change is rooted in attention and discernment. Paradoxically, when we pull focus into what we can control, when we pay attention, when we overcome our fear of being not in control, when we can place our action into small exchanges and adjustments, only then, over time and with consistent application, can we bend the arc of our experience and our reality. Little change, consistently applied, can add up.

To implement change in your own situation, bring the attention very local, into the body and one's immediate physical and emotional condition. What do we need to obtain, be, act as, and do to recalibrate energy and being? Is it worth repeating? Are our expectations for the result occurring? What is different now, and does it bring greater equilibrium or contentment or pleasure and less pain? Or is the pain we're experiencing that of a purifying kind? If so, proceed; if not, readjust.

To change the world, we must pay attention and make exchanges, alterations, and amendments one step at a time. We mutate to match our surroundings and conditions. In that, change is constant, but change is hard because paying attention and living in the moment, right here and now, is hard. But that is our task: change. Right-sized, right-purposed, and right-directed.

Change is constant. Change is hard. And change is our purpose in life. We think we can change by reaction and inattention. But the transformation happens with attention, action, and purpose.

On Birds, Trees, Flowers, and Owls

The first thing I really noticed after we went into shelter-in-place were the blossoms on the trees. It was late March or early April, and the trees were laden with flowers. Around the reservoir in Central Park were dozens of white-, pink-, and red-flowered trees in bloom, all casting off an admixture of delicate scents. Every day the flowers grew bigger, and the tree branches drooped further ever so slightly. In the backyard of my apartment building there was a magnolia tree in full bloom. This magnolia was the outdoors thing I saw most frequently and was often the only hint that there was an outside anywhere during the first weeks of the pandemic. This tree gave me hope.

I would sit at my window and contemplate: Were the trees always this resplendent? Was it just this year as a result of a relatively warm winter, or were the trees always so beautiful and I had not noticed before? And if I hadn't noticed before, why not? These reflections would get me curious.

Next: birds. First, I heard them. One early morning I poked my head out the door to look up at the sky. The city was eerily silent, it being too early for the wail of sirens that would occupy daytime hours. The piercing screech of a seagull sliced the air. I remembered then that New York is a maritime city. The gull reminded me that the ocean surrounded and embraced us, and that Manhattan has a geography that can be easy to overlook or forget in the tight warren of streets and high-rises. The presence of the powerful, vibrant ocean so close was somehow comforting.

As the sun rose earlier each day, I woke earlier and walked in Central Park. I noticed robins, their bright red tummies revealing them as they hopped on the ground. I welcomed them back, thinking that they signified warmer weather and the passing of time, both happy omens in the context of a pandemic. As the season passed deeper into spring and the trees unfolded their flowers, the panic over the city relaxed its grip. The robins hopped on, unfazed.

Then, one afternoon: the magic of a blue jay. By late spring the vines that wrapped themselves across the brick on my building bore tasty fruit and were visited almost daily by a single jay. I would look up from my computer screen and see the jay perched on the vine, snapping at the dark berries. It was indifferent to me, focused on its task. The feathers on the top of its head ruffled in the breeze. I was reminded that things carried on, and that I needed to get out of my own head.

I started to see cardinals and finches everywhere. During my walks in Central Park, they emerged from every corner. I saw sparrows, crows, cardinals, redwing blackbirds, warblers, thrushes, finches, and chickadees. I'd stop and play with tufted titmice that ate from my hand. I came to know woodpeckers, herons, egrets, and ducks of several varieties. And I saw loons in the pond. Some days, I would sit on a bench and just watch the birds. And listen to birdsong and melody, and the rustling of leaves and feathers. There was so much life available in such a confined space; there was magic and mystery in diversity. Their activity could be my relaxation and calm.

I found the bird feeders in the Ramble, as well as the bird whisperers. I would walk up silently behind a bird watcher with her binoculars trained on a tree branch to see what was there. I got better at seeing clusters of people and understanding when they were gathered to watch something that gets airborne. I learned to see the tops of trees and the birds of prey that lived there. Central Park has a number of red-tailed hawks, and I started to see them often. On my runs around the ring road, I would see them on the East Drive landing in trees or taking off. Although I have run in Central Park for half a decade, I have seen more red-tailed hawks in three months than in the previous three years. Why is that? Over time, the sight of the hawks grew more astounding as I started to interpret their behavior. I was often stopped in my tracks, in awe.

But what caught my eye most were the ground flowers, both those planted in the gardens and ones just blooming everywhere. How did it ever come to be that there were so many flowers? At first, bright tulips and astounding white lilies caught my eye as I walked around the reservoir. I loved the yellows and oranges and pinks and reds. Then I discovered the Shakespeare Garden. I don't know the half of what flowers I saw, but I couldn't stop taking photographs. Every week there was a different tapestry of flora, and I was treated to a kaleidoscope of colors. Why did I let so many years go by before remarking how many shades of purple petals can exist in nature in such close proximity?

And scents. Although I had been advised to stop and smell the flowers, I am not certain I ever really had before. Or, at least, not so frequently. How it is that flowers can smell like flowers but also like fruit? How did I not notice that the smell in the air changes not only with the season, but even week to week as different flowers, grasses, and leaves grow? How did I not notice that flowers are most fragrant at dawn and dusk, and that humidity can both dampen and enrich a sweet smell?

After almost a year, I can really start not only to look but also to see, including seeing things that don't want to be seen. This is the gift of the owl. At dusk in deepest winter, I was walking through the Ramble and felt it. I stopped, then noticed the outline of other people standing still off to one side, and so I waited. It took my eyes some time to focus in the darkening light, but there it was: an owl moved silently from one branch to another about fifty feet away. It landed with its back to us, and there it sat, immobile. We waited as the night closed in around us, and I believed that I could just make out its head swiveling. I imagined that the owl looked directly at me. That may have happened.

It seems to me that I recently experienced a perfect circle. While on a long run, an avid and gifted birder brought some of us to see a barred owl. I am better trained at seeing things I look at now, so I was able to spot it high up in a tree. It was fifty feet up and sat still. Before this year I would not have seen it. It was, simply, too big to see; I couldn't have imaged a bird being that size, so I would not have seen it. This year has taught me to know that birds are there and to allow my eyes to relax and see them. These trees, birds, and flowers have taught me well. Now I can see something I might have missed before, both because I was unable to look for it and because in my busy life I may have lacked the patience and curiosity to go looking for something like a big owl in Central Park. The next day I brought a different running friend there to the same tall tree. The experience was magical. The barred owl was exactly where I said it was; I described the tree and the position of the bird exactly. Together with some birders, we stared in wonder.

All these moments have brought me peace and a renewed appreciation for attention. In seeing the blossoms of the trees and the variety of birds and the vibrancy of the flowers, I've had to focus and pay detailed attention to what is around me. What the natural world has gifted me this year has been to teach my eyes to see the splendor of the physical world rather than staying distracted by the abstract worries that have so often previously preoccupied me.

After this past year, I understand that life, to be lived, compels us to revel in attention and not to shut any of it out: the good, the bad, the pain, or the joy. The purpose of life is to learn to live it more fully and with greater attention.

To live life tree by tree, bird by bird, flower by flower. And one magnificent owl at a time.

On Overwhelm

I'm convinced a lot of panic or anxiety that people feel has overwhelm at its root. Overwhelm can be a powerful emotion, and more so because it is characterized as an action rather than as a transient state. As a culture, we do not give overwhelm its credit except in a limited range of contextual situations such as terror. But if we can recognize when we are beset by feelings of overwhelm and acknowledge and feel them, many of the consequences of the emotion, such as paralysis or meltdowns, are moderated.

We mostly use *overwhelm* as a transitive verb: when we do so, it must have a direct object. It is a verb that acts upon someone or something. A dictionary will suggest that its most prevalent meaning is associated with overthrow or upset. It can also have meanings associated with being overpowered, submerged, or subsumed; all of these words signify having been overcome. We describe an army line or city as being overwhelmed by the enemy, or a person as being overwhelmed by grief. Water can overwhelm a place in a flood. *Overwhelm* in all of these contexts is the link between one thing or action being too much to deal with over another.

But as an emotion, overwhelm can also be a noun. When overwhelm sets in, our brains are hijacked: we may feel like we must be everywhere at once to deal with the potential of something larger than we can grasp. We are eating an elephant all in one go—and quickly. Our brains respond with a sense of emergency, which can turn on our fight-or-flight systems, and which can trigger sensations or thoughts that may be too much to handle all at once.

Overwhelm, in this sense, is like the Microsoft Blue Screen of Death, when the system is hung up because it has too much to process and is missing a key instruction. It's an operating error, but one that provides information if we can pause to recognize and interpret it. Fight or flight is the physiological experience of overwhelm, and our human equivalent of a processing error. But there is an emotional component too, and I've come to believe that overwhelm is also a distinct and unique emotional state that we all need to do a better job of acknowledging. That sensation of fight or flight comes as a package of feels. If we slow down the image speed and put on the freeze-frame to really look at it, we can recognize that the feeling is there to nudge us and show us something.

I experience the emotion of overwhelm both as a sudden activation of alertness that occurs at the same time as, and in tension with, a complete and comprehensive fatigue. Overwhelm can feel at once like a flood and like falling from a cavernous height. The immediate onset of overwhelm can literally take my breath away. This is all hardly surprising: what is likely happening is that some part of my brain thinks it is being attacked and is activating a lot of chemicals in an effort to get my attention. But it's how we harness attention in that micro-moment that can matter to what happens next and how we react.

It's not surprising to me that symptoms of overwhelm are often paralysis or meltdowns, and meltdowns can often leave adults behaving like toddlers. The feeling of over-whelm can make us feel like the world is suddenly too big, out of control, and scary. That's overwhelm in action. In the moment of overwhelm, we hold on to the illusion that we can somehow control what's going on, or that events in the world can be organized and understood. When we let that go, when we acknowledge that big and bad things will happen unexpectedly sometimes whether or not we'd like them to, we can shift our focus to the only thing we can control: our reactions to those events.

This is, in effect, much of the work of growing up: just acknowledging that all of it is too much of a mess and, de-spite it all, proceeding anyway by developing mastery over our minds and emotions. Overwhelm is the emotion that can give us key information to help us recognize when to disengage and revert to the thinking mind. Overwhelm, by its force, is an alarm system sent to warn us. Like all emotions, overwhelm is a messenger: it's one of the body's crucial pathways of sending out important information.

If we don't recognize what overwhelm is trying to com-municate and that we must detach, we become entangled in the underlying events. We identify ourselves with the operating error of trying to process too much information rather than slowing down the processing or rebooting. If our thinking mind doesn't disengage, we become tangled up in those powerful chemical impulses and are carried along with them, rather than acknowledging that we only have our perceptions of things and our actions to govern us. Emotions are just information. They are transitory and will pass if we let ourselves process them. Let overwhelm be our cue and our teacher, rather than our outcome.

On Perspective

This morning I'm on the tenth floor of a building facing west. I watched the sun rise through its reflection in the windows across from me. As morning deepens and the sky turns a darker shade of pale blue and clouds dot the sky, I think about this perspective and how the city appears different from a height.

From above, I see people walking on the sidewalks and going about their business. Across from me is a market, and the workers are on the sidewalk stocking fruit and other items in baskets in neat rows outside the store. Despite the snow and ice, intrepid cyclists skid down the middle of the road. The early morning delivery trucks have disappeared and been replaced by near-empty city buses and some cars. There is a grocery service delivery truck parked outside the produce section of the market, in a comical juxtaposition of modern shopping modes.

It snowed heavily in the city two days ago, and it is snowing again. There is a different experience of snow from ten stories high. Up here, the wind can still catch the snow before it has completed its free fall and whip it about. As I watched the sun rise, I also watched the snow fly up the side of the building. It was not a snowfall, but a snow-up. It was gorgeous.

I see how snow lines the roof of a building opposite. I see water towers everywhere. The ingenuity of New Yorkers is apparent. Tucked into corners of building blocks are terraces and Juliet balconies, conservatories built into the sides of buildings, and a cabana on a rooftop, all there to help New Yorkers get a view and some air. I imagine the views from some of these landings are remarkable: it would be possible to see the Hudson River or the city or Central Park or all three views at once.

A different view is, of course, a different perspective, which offers both a literal and metaphorical new way of seeing. From high up the city looks different than it does at street level. So, too, the way we look at things in our circumstances can be different if we shift our position. For example, when I enlarge my view by traveling ten stories up, all my personal problems seem smaller by comparison, and for some reason I don't understand, I assign them less weight. Perhaps it's because my field of vision is more expansive, and so I am better able to right-size my own self-perception, or that the view from a height somehow makes everything seem more manageable.

Height is one form of gaining perspective; time is another. I experience life as a sort of Möbius loop; events and people and emotions return, but slightly differently. Each time an aspect of life revisits me on the loop, I see it anew. The people I knew in a previous time are fundamentally the same now, but weathered or wiser. Circumstances or emotions I've previously experienced return to me, frayed and familiar, and sometimes a revisited feeling occurs more intensely. When something unexpected emerges, the perspective of time places it within an ever-longer context. I know now with certainty that, given some time, whatever this is shall pass. What we are really talking about when we talk about the wisdom of the ages is the wisdom that age brings, because of the new relationship with the perspective of time.

Perspective brings distance, the kind of distance that acts as a form of separation that precludes immersion but highlights relationship. I see that I am here, relative to there. I see that this is now, relative to then. I can see how the parts fit, and how I fit into the parts.

Like any information learned but not studied, I sat through a course on the history of painting, but almost all the subject matter is now completely lost to me. I remember a lecture about the invention of perspective in Western painting and how important that was. I can no longer remember the significance the instructor placed on this, but I can recall how the art used to illustrate this advancement differed sharply from what we had just studied: the introduction of perspective into painting made the depictions seem more lifelike. The images were more proportioned, geometric, realistic, and less stylized. With perspective, people and objects could be grouped differently within a canvass or tapestry, and so artists were using the space and the field innovatively. Different stories were able to be told, and different interpretations could become available because different relationships could be depicted through perspective.

This opportunity I've had this week, this new perspective, has helped me reenter the city. During the pandemic,

I've been ensconced in my garden apartment, literally underground. But from this height, it's possible to feel reborn, and it's impossible to not understand that one is but a small moving part in a huge city. To see both what is permanent and impermanent. Smoke rises from a chimney and disperses against a pale blue sky. I am looking at this now and can imagine someone fifty years ago looking at the exact same thing, from exactly this vantage point. There is much outside this window that would be the same now as then, even though many things would be different.

From this location ten stories up, I've shifted my view and shifted myself emotionally. I'm marking this moment with these words as a reminder that new perspectives are valuable and to seek them out constantly. Whether it's the perspective of a new location, a new view, or a new voice, new ways of seeing and being give us distance from the immersion of our own worldview, which we can mistake for the only available reality. We are always enriched by perspective. We become more nuanced and able to group ourselves and things differently in relation to each other. Perspective is maturation of our being in the world.

On Procrastination

I've carried a few tasks and errands forward for several days in my journal. I've found myself wondering this morning whether I'm procrastinating on doing these things and, if so, why.

Procrastination is an act of delaying or postponing a task or set of tasks, usually by rationalizing it will get done "tomorrow" or "later" but without scheduling the time to do it. The key here is that procrastination *is* an act; it is the choice to delay while knowing that the underlying thing needs to get done and that there could be negative consequences to this delay. Procrastination can feel passive because it involves not doing something, but it often takes work and requires reserves of mental energy. There are times when I have spent days acting on procrastination, only to eventually complete the underlying task in a few minutes. I've devoted significant mental energy both into rationalizing the avoidance and excoriating myself for engaging in procrastination at all.

Procrastinators are sometimes characterized as lazy, less productive, or as having negative traits such as inadequacy or low self-esteem. But there's a flip side too: procrastination can result from cautiousness, or its most serious incarnation, perfectionism, in an effort to avert a negative outcome or to wait for more or better information. There can be a quiet wisdom in some procrastination. For example, I can put off doing errands with the best of them. I believe I've raised procrastination to an art form. But in this, I can be too hard on myself. I'm also remarkably busy and tend to be very effective in getting things done, so procrastination for me can just be a self-defense mechanism to rest.

But I've also discovered a relationship between when I procrastinate and my priorities. A priority is something in the state of bring prior, or before. That suggests that a priority is a thing I should do first. But I tend to put off things that aren't priorities, so I can also find an internal logic to much of my procrastination.

But priorities are personal. And here is where things get complicated: sometimes something I need to do is a priority for me, but urgent or quotidian matters may need to supersede my doing them. Or more troubling, something that's a priority really does call to me, but I put it off because I feel guilty or bad about getting to it, usually in advance of something else I feel I should be doing but that doesn't call to me with the same tenor or tone. I can want to spend all day walking around in the park daydreaming or spend time in the city looking at buildings, but something on my to-do list is underlined as important; I may end up putting off that underlined task but feel too guilty to daydream, so I just spend the day doing nothing, neither getting the work done nor stimulating my imagination.

I don't think I'm alone in doing this or behaving this way.

I wonder whether procrastination is cultural and is a symptom of our ever-switched-on, fix-it-at-all-costs culture. We are told we can have it all, but we are not really taught how to want things that are unique or meaningful to us. Because we are generally all taught to want everything, we are taught to *do* everything, so a to-do list can become long, and such a list will inevitably include activity that is actually unnecessary to our well-being. As a result, we confuse what we want with what we need, and end up needing what we are ingrained to want. In such a state, it is hard if not impossible to prioritize, to choose what goes first, and to select one thing from many on which to focus our time and attention.

Awareness and focus are the antidotes to this frenetic state of being, by allowing me to deliberately choose to do less. With fewer things on the to-do list, it becomes easier for me to distinguish what I am really putting off from that which I just don't have time to do. I now choose three things a day, each day, that I must do, and permit others to fall into another day.

It is more often the case that I accomplish everything on my list every day because I have planned and prioritized, which may hint at a key to unlocking the malaise of our time: the absence of prioritization. We so very rarely prioritize; instead, we plan. These are not the same thing, because we can make a plan to do something that isn't a priority. Or we can plan something that isn't something we need to do first. When we put off something that is a priority for us, we add noise to our lives, whether it is a use of time or emotional energy. We can experience this noise as depression, anxiety, or burnout.

For me, the key to leading a happier, more balanced life has been by paying attention to when I procrastinate and inquiring why, and then acting on that awareness. If I am avoiding a necessary task, I ask *why*. If I intuit that I need more information before doing something, I take a step to get that information. If I am pausing because I really don't want to do the task, I determine whether it really needs to be done. If it does, I'll schedule it; if it doesn't, I'll drop it or delegate it. And in whole areas of human activity that I've decided aren't priorities for me, I spend less time and energy.

I procrastinate less often now, but when I do, I more often consider my awareness of this inclination to be a gift. Procrastination can be a signpost or a guide to right-action, to aligning action with intention, and focusing our energy.

On Burnout

It's been a year. In New York City we are a year into this pandemic, and today marks one year to the day since the first death from COVID-19 was recorded. Everywhere around me I see signs of burnout, or the denial or avoidance of signs of burnout. I see the latter as meta-level burnout, which is itself a symptom of burnout. Sometimes the experience of burnout is so overwhelming its existence must be denied or avoided to be survived.

I speculate that the term *burnout* is borrowed from rocket science. I first learned about this term when I was a teenager and enthusiastically watched space shuttle launches. Burnout is when a jet engine or rocket ceases to operate because of fuel exhaustion or shutoff. More generally, mechanical burnout occurs when there is a failure in a device caused by burning, heat, or excessive friction. Engines will burn out. Lawnmowers will burn out. Treadmills will burn out (if they are used).

But most people use the term *burnout* to refer to a state of emotional, mental, and physical exhaustion brought about by prolonged or repeated stress. We refer to such a state as "burnout" and a person experiencing burnout as "running on fumes" as if they were booster rockets. Often the conceit relates to work, believing that burnout is a function of an unhappy or unfulfilling job or a difficult boss, since stress at work can be chronic and, in our culture, we spend so much time there. But people can experience burnout by other phenomena such as illness, challenging relationships, or even family or self-driven expectations. Or a person can have too many overlapping responsibilities, such as paid employment and unpaid family care, or be in a situation that exacerbates stress, such as toxic relationships, abuse, or poverty.

Or burnout may follow a year of living through a once-in-a-generation pandemic and the dislocation to routines—and for some, job losses and family disruption—that this has caused. I know that recently I have been sleeping a lot and recognize this as a coping mechanism and an attempt to stave off burnout. What I really want is the stimulation of serendipity: spending an immersive afternoon in a gallery, sitting on a bench and watching a street performer, enjoying a beverage at an outdoor café and watching throngs of passersby, and heading out to a concert or show. I'm lucky: my burnout is mostly one of isolation and lack of extraordinary inputs. Others have burnout that roots from much lower down in Maslow's hierarchy of needs.

Some of us may think of burnout loosely as a kind of temporary mental illness. Individuals may experience burnout in isolation and as a period of loss of interest in activities or exhaustion. They may conflate it with a kind of light depression. The popular literature, including media articles about burnout, may reinforce this view by providing checklists of symptoms to look for, as though burnout is primarily a health issue and a personal one to be discussed with a doctor or therapist.

I am skeptical of this view of burnout and think it is dangerous and may promote harm. Among the symptoms of burnout, beyond exhaustion, is a cynicism and disillusionment often accompanied by a loss of enthusiasm for activities. Many people who are experiencing burnout withdraw or fall away, like booster rockets. And this too: burnout can contribute to a lowering of self-esteem, which in turn can engender feelings of self-doubt and loss of confidence in one's skills and abilities. We often locate burnout in the sufferer's tendencies to take on too much, be a perfectionist, a caretaker, or some other personal attribute; and the person experiencing burnout may be particularly prone to adopt or live through this view if they are too exhausted or overwhelmed to consider the meaning and implication of such statements. A characteristic of burnout is that the cultural modality is to both blame the sufferer for the burnout and place uniquely on their shoulders the responsibility for remediating it, either by "demonstrating resiliency" or by withdrawing, such as removing themselves from the workplace, relationship, or situation.

Instead, consider the contexts from which we have borrowed the term *burnout*. In rocket science, burnout occurs by design and is a function of the system; burnout of the rocket booster may be necessary to the effective design of the overall system. In mechanics, burnout may also be a characteristic of the design of the machine or may be indicative of lack of maintenance or overuse of one element within the system or machine.

Burnout is systemic and often a result of design.

Stressed out by your job? Perhaps, by design, there is too much work and not enough resources, or insufficient or too much automation, leaving you feeling dislocated from the inputs and outputs. Or the stated purpose of the work is misaligned with interests or aptitudes, and no one is responsible for fixing it. Or the pay is misaligned with experience or risk. Or we have a system of commuting to offices and property ownership based around transportation and taxation systems in need of an overhaul.

Stressed out by a relationship? Is it the relationship or the systems of support for that relationship that are broken? Perhaps, by design, families are atomized, communities are fractured, and children are locked into relentless competitions for access to schools, education, leisure, and credentials that require ample parental time and participation. Family units are venerated but are also isolated and stressed, by design, without social and governmental infrastructure.

Stressed out by existential angst? A lack of purpose? Increasingly within our culture, we are told to follow our idiosyncratic bliss, but humans are social mammals and most find purpose in community and being helpful to others. We are taught to substitute social standing for social service and then wonder at the epidemic of loneliness.

Repeat it again: burnout is systemic and reveals the limits of system design. In my experience, burnout results when the social supports around a person fail and the person is left to fend for themselves. At work it may be from having too much responsibility or activity and insufficient support, or there is a dislocation between what someone intends to do and how they spend their time. And burnout often follows this pattern: "I intend to help people, but instead I am just filling out forms/driving in circles/watching people die, unable to intervene or help."

People burn out because we treat them like booster rockets: we let them use up their fuel and then hope they will separate and cast themselves away—into the ocean! Or we leave the person unattended, effectively allowing their parts to wear down, overheat, or experience too much friction as stress, or fail to update their resources, training, or experience. Like a part in a machine, such a human will eventually wear down and potentially burn out.

Culturally we are experiencing burnout at this year marker of the pandemic, but we must not believe the burnout is a result solely of the time spent. We are experiencing burnout because, despite the time that's passed, we find ourselves within systems that are exposed as worn out, as burning up, having too much heat and friction. Our hospital and unemployment and job-filling systems are frayed, our elected governments have not functioned as needed, our schools are exposed largely as failures, and many other systems and institutions are under strain. It's exhausting to think about, the work to be done in fixing it all.

But the heat and failure of burnout call attention to what isn't working. In the sudden jolt of the pandemic's arrival, some things changed quickly and unexpectedly for the better. But we need to remember burnout is systemic, and we should not become convinced that burnout is a personal issue to be dealt with alone or quietly.

Let's use this year as a magnifying glass to look at everything that contributes to our stress and exhaustion and consider whether this system is designed to wear down any resistance to it. Or is it just past its best-before date or not well maintained? Many of our systems were designed in a previous century to tackle problems that are in our culture's rearview mirror; the component parts may just be old and in need of replacement. The systems themselves may be burnt out. Instead of taking it all on ourselves, we should hold the systems that contribute to our burnout to account. And in some cases, we might want to shift the understanding of what's burnt out to systems and ensure the parts that are still needed are replaced.

On Destruction

When I opened the box, I found my glass vase and pitcher shattered. I could tell immediately, without fully unwrapping them, that they were broken, as the paper surrounding them had lost form. When I tried to lift the lumpen shape from the box, I heard the distinctive tinkling sound of glass falling against glass.

Both vessels were on the smaller side, and the glass used to make them was not as thick as that of the other glass items they were packed with, so perhaps they were frailer. But they had also been packed loosely with large wooden items that were not wrapped, and the moving box into which they were placed was only partly full, meaning the items could have shifted (and likely did) during transportation. Their destruction, under these circumstances, was unsurprising.

A part of me, in that moment of discovery, was sad. I had attached good memories to these objects. I had used the glass pitcher to hold water at work so I wouldn't have to get up during the day to get more, and more recently, I had used it to steep iced tea. I used the vase to hold tulips because it was just the right size for a small bouquet. I love tulips and had used this vase often.

There is something so final in the destruction of a glass object. Glass fragments are beautiful, but their multitude of pieces reveal the practical complexity of reassembly. And because shards of glass themselves shatter, the possibility of repair back into the original is illusory. When other items break, such as those made of wood, metal, or fabric, the tear, fraying, or break often happens such that the way to fix the item is immediately visible. Less so with glass.

To destroy an object is to reduce it to useless fragments, to injure it beyond repair, to render it ineffective, or to put an end to it. So, too, with destruction of an adversary: a man is destroyed when killed, neutralized, or defeated completely. Destruction requires activity and action. It is not a passive process, even when the destroyed object is acted upon. Destruction does not always take intention or forethought, but it does take energy.

But as I reflected on my vase and pitcher, I realized that their destruction likely resulted from lack of intention or forethought. A little more care in packing, whether in wrapping them or placing them in the box, might have resulted in their safe and effective transportation. While a human hand did not directly result in their destruction, the lack of human intervention in planning and care created the conditions in which other forces in the box could act on them destructively.

This may be true of so much destruction. It is easy to focus on direct human acts, such as war, violence, and anger, as key contributors to and causes of the loss. We focus on the active agents in cases of destruction: on the person who started the fire that burned down the block, or the person whose finger pulled the trigger of the gun, or on the actions and skill level of the driver of the vehicle involved in a crash. But in doing so we may diagnose only part of the problem and tell the lesser part of the story. Much destruction results from inaction and lack of care or inattention too. Or destruction can result from a lack of consequences for avoiding action.

When we see destruction only through the lens of activity, we remove from consideration thoughts about training, design, process, and power in the systems that underpin that action and that generate scope of autonomy. In focusing solely on the actor of the destruction, we fail to consider the context in which that actor acted, making the destruction possible. Did they have access to the tools of destruction? Did others notice the potential for violence or aggressive action and fail to act themselves? Did policies uniquely disempower the victims, increasing the likelihood of their loss and effectively shifting the risk onto persons less able to bear it? Often we create systems and structures that enable acts of destruction and then are shocked when those acts occur.

These musings also apply to destruction arising from natural or nonhuman situations such as hurricanes or other natural disasters. While it's true that such things will happen, what role did seemingly passive human decisions have in contributing to the destruction? Does an insurance policy encourage risky building? Is poverty contributing to the placement of communities in harm's way or limiting the resources to build better and stronger? Do our communities just not want to organize themselves to grapple with the task of complex problem-solving and, if so, why?

The way we look at destruction affects how we account for it and how we bring what caused it to account. When we consider that destruction occurs within a complex of action and decisions supported by many, the passive or invisible contributors to destruction may be revealed. The chain of contribution—indirect, sometimes unseen, usually pervasive—is foregrounded. But often, despite being revealed, this chain of contribution is ignored. It is not always possible to understand how or how much each of the elements of the complex of actions contributed to the loss, which is possibly why their role is sometimes not measured at all. How to apportion fault when it's difficult to map out the role and contribution of the person who chose not to get involved? Or to tease out how the policy, long in the books and which appears to be too difficult to change, could have yielded a different outcome if it had been previously modified?

But we can understand that even micro-changes could have an impact. Not everything needs to change, and sometimes changing just one item in the complex of factors can make a difference, reduce risk, and decrease destructive capacity. Had my vase and pitcher been even slightly better wrapped, I might still have something into which I could place tulips. But I would also not have meditated on how things can get destroyed by inaction, and I might not have been catalyzed to remember to look beyond the immediate destruction and to use new eyes to try and see what might really be going on.

On Foundations

I have two old pairs of running shoes sitting in the hallway that are waiting for me to recycle them at the running store when I go to pick up another pair. My running shoe store is part of a network that collects running shoes that have been over-loved by distance and sends them to a company that breaks down the rubber, which is then used to make cinder tracks. I love the idea that my running shoes can go from supporting me and my feet to becoming the foundation of runs under the feet of others across the country.

These shoes built the foundation for my current fitness. Each of them covered a lot of territory as I ramped up my mileage base between November and January. I bought a lighter pair of shoes than I usually wear and used these to log one or two extra runs a week beyond my normal training mileage. For the first time in years, I'm often running six days a week. Now that the distance is there, I'm layering in short, intense running work called intervals. The speed, such as it is at my age, is starting to come back. I'm not doing too much too fast, and my body is able to adapt to the increased stress.

I'm a lifelong runner, and while I have been running for the past few years, I haven't done so with the same frequency, intensity, or ease as in years past. It's taken me a long time to return to the level of fitness that I'm currently enjoying. A key to running is the base, or the foundation, on which everything else gets layered. An effective base is a certain level of strength in the body, plus an aerobic capacity achieved by running, often relatively slowly. The activity of running improves with preparation before each individual run, and in preparation more generally; the body is best prepared to run by previous running.

Indeed, anyone who moves past recreational running into understanding it as an avocation—something to which some serious time and mental energy is devoted— will quickly come to realize that for all its spontaneity, running can be a planful preoccupation. To embark upon a training journey, for example, by registering for a race sometime in the future, is to learn the mysteries and science of training plans for runners: of breaking up training into pieces of work and undertaking those pieces in a purposeful way so that each builds on the next, shaping the body and mind into a whole greater than the sum of the parts. Training for longer distances, such as the half or full marathon, are tackled this way. Marathon training in particular is built on a base of many miles.

Running teaches you that showing up is a process and that this process, when undertaken with patience and dedication, can build to unexpected and unimaginable achievements. For many runners, the process is as much the reward as the race itself. I can find my greatest enjoyment in those daily runs, in knowing that this habit will scratch the itch of getting out there and feeling alive.

It's said that most of winning is about showing up. As I've aged, I've realized that this saying is not about a single moment nor about moments of chance or luck. Instead, it's a reminder that anything worthwhile is built on a foundation, even if we don't see it, and that establishing a foundation takes time, discipline, and focus. It's about showing up not once, but over and over again. Building a running base requires logging miles, including in rain, in the morning when you'd rather be in bed, and on days when you're fed up. It's passing through "character-building runs," which are generally not glorious but prime the body and mind to confront adversity. If I run one morning when it's windy and rainy, I'm more likely to do it again, and more likely to not get daunted and go out anyway when I encounter a cold, drizzly morning with gale-force winds on a scheduled race day, as I did the morning of a marathon that I ran anyway. I turned in a personal record performance because I drew upon a reserve established during my running foundation.

What we do matters. How we do it also matters. How we spend our time shapes our minds and bodies and primes our relationships and our neural pathways. We are always laying foundations, even though we may not be aware we are doing so. We are what we do because this is how we are being.

Understanding the importance of foundations is critical to identifying where additional time and resources may be helpful. All experience shapes foundations, but painful experiences may shape the base in an unhelpful way. Lessons learned as children, through negative experiences or mistakes in apprehension may put a foundation down in a place that's unhelpful, like building on quicksand. We might have had experiences that shape an unhelpful view of who we are (*I'm unlovable*), an unhelpful view of our capabilities (*I can't do that*), or an unhelpful understanding of our opportunities (*I shouldn't do that*). Renovating a foundation is hard but not impossible: we renovate houses and wardrobes after all, and we can use therapy or religious faith to help us renovate our emotional capacity or belief structures. Like renovating a house, renovating the foundation of a life involves taking a clear view of the current structure, developing a plan for transformation, and putting in the work. There are bound to be surprises along the way, but a foundation set down years before can undergo uplift and reinforcement.

I've been examining my foundations recently, holding up to scrutiny what inputs I take in and taking an accounting of the things I've spent time on. We have so little time on this planet, even if we live a long, healthy life, that every moment is an opportunity to root a little deeper into the structure of our lives. In myself, I see years of dreaming rather than doing and times when I've introduced distracting habits, substantial dislocation, and rework. But I also see evidence through the years of consistency, routine, and practice at a few things learned slowly and well. I've established deep foundations in travel, reading, writing, curiosity, and creativity for problem-solving. I've developed the capacity to travel far, over distance, with stamina. I've thought deeply about a few things, and I may even be cultivating a bit of wisdom about how to take people with me over long, difficult journeys.

The miles my running shoes have logged are paying off and will continue to do so.

What has served me well on my journey through life is returning again and again to the activities that forge my foundation: running, traveling, and writing. My relationship with each of these activities goes beyond love and hate. They are so foundational in that I do them now regardless of how I feel about them, and my identity and being make no sense to me without the doing of them. I run, therefore I am; I am, therefore I run. I write, therefore I am; I am, therefore I write. As I return to my foundation again and again, I discover who I am, and create myself into being.

When I don't think I have anything to say, I look at my notebooks, and my fingers find words on this keyboard. When I don't think I can take another step, the running shoes in my closet remind me that I have and can travel far, and that I will travel farther. When my vision is cloudy and obscured, or when I am beset by doubts and paralysis, I look at the art on my walls and understand I will perceive clearly and differently when I look to *see*. I know that I'll pick out the shapes and contours for the action that I'll need.

It's about foundations, about the base of who we are, built moment by moment in what we do.

On Cowardice

This week I started to take steps to do something that I find scary. I had been paralyzed in decision-making about a situation that required action for some time, and I finally had to break the activity down into micro-steps and just get started. Now that I've started taking action with my very first small and tentative step, I can start to see a path clear through what, even a month ago, was a fog of dread—or a fog of cowardice that caused me great anxiety.

It is commonly said that cowardice emerges as a trait when a person is paralyzed by fear, in order to avoid facing danger or taking a risk. Cowardice lies in opposition to courage on this spectrum if we understand courage as being afraid but acting anyway. But why do some succumb to fear while others do not? Can courage be taught or developed?

I've been thinking about this a lot, including meditating on my root cause of being stuck and identifying what shifted that enabled me to take action where before there was paralysis. I know what I was afraid of and what caused me anxiety about the situation. But why couldn't I act? What changed for me? It wasn't just the breaking down of the task into little pieces. It was the commitment of deciding to start and then acting.

Commitment unlocks action because it is a promise or a firm decision to do something. Commitment occurs when one has thought through various scenarios and chosen one. There is a quality of being fixed in a course of action associated with the word. A commitment to a marriage, a team, a position, or an institution conjures the image of staying the course, despite what happens.

In other words, commitment is action that arises from a plan. That plan can be a decision. It can also be practice, whether rehearsed or arising from visualization. A plan from commitment can also arise within faith or philosophy, both of which ground action because they train the mind to see in a particular way and respond accordingly.

Understood this way, acting according to a plan can be an antidote to fear. Courage may arise not from ignoring fear but metabolizing it within a larger image of what is possible, including locating action from a place of agency. Because I can see what I intend to do as a result of my plan, it is easier to continue on with it, and to adapt when things don't exactly go my way. The person we understand to be courageous may simply be a person with a more practiced sense of the way forward.

To discover courage may involve cultivating intentionality in things. Intentionality is awareness and purpose. It is a state of having been formed by a resolution to act consciously and by design. Courage, then, is a state evolved from intentionality, and cowardice may simply be the manifestation of a lack of intentionality.

I can think of situations where I believed that my courage had failed me. But I see also that in such situations I was not prepared and that I was destabilized by that lack of preparation when an event required a modification that I had no bandwidth to address. I have been in meetings where something was said that I disagreed with, but I could not find my voice, either because I had not anticipated the topic raised or did not understand the power dynamics or cultural context. I have been cowardly about taking risks because I didn't have intentionality about what I was trying to accomplish. With a plan, it is easier to adapt as new people, events, and possibilities arise.

That cowardice may be related to an absence of intentionality is clarifying because it suggests that we all are capable of courage in all things if we take the time to develop planful action. And it helps to diagnose some of the malaise of our time, as we are beset from all sides by communications seeking to sell us things and usurp our time. It can be challenging to sort through that noise and settle on an authentic, intentional path. When we are not steering by using our own intention and vision, we can be subject to inaction or simply following the loudest pathway delivered to us. Automation has a kind of power to it too, but one born of momentum rather than desire. Roadblocks and confusion are likely to unsettle and derail it.

Taking the time and effort to establish intention is not only clarifying; it is powerful. It points toward action, grounds decision, and catalyzes courage. Too often we assume that intention is additive and requires a decision to add more and to do more. But the most magical and graceful action may arise from subtraction, when we sort through all possibilities but settle on those that are meaningful to us. Intentionality requires choice. It means prioritizing some actions over others.

But when we know what we want, have planned how we might get there, and envision who we need to be on the journey, our convictions are established: we discover magic and grace in the action of moving toward the goal. And we can also discover that in consistent forward motion toward a goal rooted in intention is where courage and grace may lie, waiting to be released.

On Revolutions

It's been just over a year since the pandemic tsunami washed over me here in New York City. Since then I've had a full revolution around the sun. Last year at this time, I was tentatively emerging from strict indoor isolation and taking early morning solo walks in the half dark. It was a rainy spring, and I went outside only on inclement days to avoid other people. I lived in a perpetual state of vigilance that I'm sure was terrible for my adrenals. The news cycle was agonizing. The ambulance sirens wailed nonstop. There was a field hospital less than a mile away from me…and it was literally in a field. I knew two people on ventilators fighting for their lives, and in the days to come I would learn of several more acquaintances who died alone. I think I was in shock during this whole period. One morning I turned on the news, learned that a mass grave was being dug a mile and a half away from me, and thought, *Well, that makes sense.* I didn't cry about any of this until June.

What brought me solace last year were the flowers. I started to notice shoots emerging from the ground in late March. Although it had been a warm winter, it was a cold, rainy spring, so buds appeared early but took a while to unfold into blooms. In the earliest days of the lockdown,

I'd be greeted by new lilies, forsythias, tulips, or cherry blossoms on every walk. Seeing this new life reminded me that with time would come healing. That was my psychic life preserver, helping me to hang on a little longer and keep me afloat. Time would bring and facilitate the cure itself, that I knew for certain. The unknowns were: How much time, and what would the time cost? What would we lose before we could cross to the other side?

It is a funny measure of this past year, with its unending, blurring, nonsense time, that I've delighted in the changing of the seasons. I've experienced this pandemic year as a cycle. Without commuting to distract me, I've spent my outdoor time looking at nature and slowly moving with it through the natural changes brought about by Earth's revolution around the sun.

While we think of time as linear, it's cyclical; our measure of time is marked by the orbits of the sun and moon and the similar events we observe each time one of those revolutions ends. A revolution is the time taken by a celestial body to make a complete round of its orbit. More generally, it can also mean the motion of any figure around a center or axis or the completion of a course of the period made by the regular succession of a measure of time or by a succession of similar events.

A revolution is also a sudden, radical, or complete change, such as that which brings about a fundamental change in political organization or socioeconomic conditions. In this sense, a revolution can signal a shift in paradigm, a different way of thinking about or visualizing something. Revolutions both signal and indicate a change-over in use or preference, especially of technology.

I received the first of my two-dose COVID-19 vaccine on Friday in Harlem. I took it in the muscle, high on my left arm, close to my shoulder, about two inches above the scar that resulted from one of the first vaccines I took, as an infant, for polio. Within the span of half a foot on this part of my body is the site of not just one revolution, but two. The site at which I took the polio vaccine is an angry square of scar tissue. This COVID-19 vaccine location was briefly flushed a light reddish color. It's fine now.

Both of these vaccines are scientific achievements. We marvel not only at the ability of several companies to develop a vaccine for SARS-CoV-2 in under a year, but also that some of them involve novel technology. Under-credited, too, is the remarkable advancements in genetics over the past twenty years that permitted sequencing of the virus at scale and speed, and advancements in genetic research that may have enabled rapid pinpointing and targeting of aspects of the virus's mechanics. Remarkable, too, are the manufacturing and distribution logistics, as well as the registration and scheduling computer applications underpinning the effort to vaccinate an enormous population in a short time. The vaccine delivered into my arm earlier this week is nothing short of a revolution of science, communications, logistics, and training.

This vaccine is also a revolution of community and potential. The virus and its impacts have upended so many aspects of our lives that now we have the opportunity, and perhaps even the duty, to reimagine them. Revolutions can catalyze a shift in perception, and both bring about, and are the result of, a different way of thinking about things. Much like the influenza pandemic a century ago changed how interior space was configured, this pandemic will redraw our cityscapes, transportation options, and workplaces. It already has. That future is here—it's just, as one wag has said, that it's not yet evenly distributed.

We think of revolutions only as sudden, cataclysmic events. In a political revolution, one leader is ousted and replaced with another, and that happens quickly. But more often a revolution takes longer to unfold, and its effects and long-term tail may be felt and understood only over time. The equal and opposite reaction may not occur on a linear continuum, but on a tangent or within a cycle.

I was vaccinated for polio before I could remember it happening. By that time the vaccination campaign was well into its second decade in North America and had virtually eliminated the disease. Within another decade, the case level dropped from about fifteen thousand reported cases a year to less than a hundred. The disease was declared eliminated on the North American continent a few years later.

We may forget the impact of this period. Polio struck children, and some parents did not let their children out or allow them to socialize much, a behavior that may have reinforced the notion of the atomic family over the extended family that emerged after the Second World War. There were travel and commerce bans between cities, which may have expanded automotive use over public transit. The prevalence of polio may have started to shift settlement out of cities to suburbs so that the baby boom of children could play outdoors. The mass production and distribution of polio vaccines within the United States and Canada may have spurred manufacturing and distribution capability. Who knows? Certainly not me, but I am imagining and reinterpreting history through a different lens, hunting for the impressions and faint lines that a body makes while revolving completely around on its axis.

I received my first shot in the arm, and it is the beginning of the beginning of the end for me—whatever that means. This vaccine marks a sort of start of the second part of my life, much as receiving the polio vaccine launched me into the first part of my life. And yet, it's a return: I am reminded that we may forget pandemics, but they return, over and over again. As sure as the Earth revolves around the sun, another episodic pandemic is an alternative measure of the passage of time.

On a more personal note, I decided to get this shot in Harlem, because it was the place where I first settled after I arrived in Manhattan, my head full of dreams of a literary renaissance and the Apollo. Harlem was also the place where my imaginings of what living in this city and country would be like were shattered into a million tiny fragments. Instead of pleasant artistic fantasies, in Harlem I encountered a rough gentrification, a community that didn't quite want me, scar tissue of political fights that continued to unfold, and confusion and cacophony over culture and identity. It was the place I first voted while in the country, the place I started to establish myself, and the place where I learned from others how to belong to and within the city. The city of New York has a romance about it, but it loves you back decidedly on its own terms. New York is a revolutionary: it won't conform to your vision of it, but it will enlarge and refocus how you see the world and your place in it. You can return to the same place in the city time and again, and it is always a little different, shifted just a little.

I walked through Central Park down the West Drive after my vaccination and visited some of the places in the park that had brought me solace during the last year. The sun was out, and my eyes were met by the colorful buds and pink, white, yellow, and orange flowers that were emerging after a long winter slumber. The colors competed with the sun for my attention, bringing my eyes down to the ground, to the here and now.

And being in Central Park returned my awareness to the seasonal cycle: we are starting another revolution around the sun. Reminding us that revolutions are everywhere and occur in all times, fast and slow, if we bear witness.

On Volunteering

Thirty years ago, I accompanied a worker with Big Brothers Big Sisters Canada to a small house in the suburb of Cataraqui, Ontario. Big Brothers Big Sisters is an organization that pairs volunteers with a child who could benefit from additional mentoring. In my first year of college at Queen's University in Kingston, I had signed up to volunteer with the organization as a way of getting off campus and doing something in and for the town where I now lived. After a screening that took months and a lengthy assessment process, I was—finally—about to meet the family of the little girl whom I was going to be paired with and, of course, that little girl too.

Her name was Steacy, and she had just turned nine. I was told this was a wonderful age for a Little Sister to be, but it was an age I was wholly unfamiliar with and likely not equipped to handle. When I had registered, I had asked to be paired with a teenager, someone closer to my age and so, I thought, more relatable. But the organization had a different idea for me and enthusiastically recommended Steacy as a match. I eventually and reluctantly conceded. I preferred to be matched than to continue to be in the limbo of the assessment, and the commitment was only going to be a year.

That hour in April with Steacy and her mother changed my life, although at the time I could not even begin to imagine the how and the why of it. That first meeting was, I now understand, primarily a way for the worker to assess the match and for Steacy's mother to meet me and voice her objections if she decided I wasn't a good fit. I would, of course, be hanging out with her daughter unsupervised several times a month. The final purpose of that meeting was so that I could get a sense of what I was in for.

The meeting seemed to go well enough, and within a few weeks I was formally paired with Steacy, and we started our adventures in mentoring. Today, I have few memories of those early meetings, although Steacy has more, but I seem to have made an impression. I took her to see a play being staged and performed by some friends of mine, and she remembers it to this day. We made beaded bracelets. I took her swimming and to movies. We baked a cake, and it was a disaster: while baking, I blew a fuse, which we couldn't replace, and so we ended up trying to finish baking the cake on the barbecue.

One day I took her to Dairy Queen for an ice cream cone, and we entered a sweepstakes. Improbably, I ended up winning a trip to Toronto, and I decided to take Steacy rather than a friend. She remembers parts of this trip vividly, including entering the upscale Royal York hotel and going to a Blue Jays game (in a year they won the World Series). Looking back on this trip, it was an extraordinary decision I made, to take her, a girl I was paired with on a volunteer basis, and it was an extraordinary decision that her mother made in permitting it to happen. We ended up having a blast. The next year, when I was attending college for a year in Montreal, Steacy came to visit me, and when I returned to Kingston for the next three years, we continued with the pairing. I attended her graduation from eighth grade, and she celebrated with me when I graduated, first with my undergraduate degree and then with my graduate degree. It's likely I stayed in Kingston for my graduate degree in part because Steacy was there.

Love perfects us; this is true of all love, although in our culture we prioritize the role of romantic love in self-knowledge and self-expression. Love of friends, however, is perhaps the most important testing ground for love because it is so freely given and requires an ongoing commitment. Friendship that enriches both participants across decades is among the most extraordinary love because it exists only by choice, and there are so few social conventions to support friendship as an important part of our lives.

Steacy has taught me I have reserves of patience and care I didn't know I had. Interactions with her family taught me negotiation and boundaries. Listening to her unlocked empathy, enthusiasm, and hope in me. Watching her grow, learn, and transform into a young adult inspired me to do better and be better. She is a reservoir of possibility and potential. She leads by generosity and grace. Watching her navigate decisions, increase her wisdom, and find her community and place in the world has informed my own decision-making and intentions. I know she wants the best for me, and that encourages me, always. I become determined to live out my best qualities, and to shape our world into something I desire for her to have and want to entrust to her. Steacy's being in the world reminds me to focus on what I can control and seek to improve it as best I can.

A volunteer is a person who performs or offers to perform a service volitionally; often a volunteer is a person who works without pay or assumes an obligation to which he or she is not a party or otherwise invested. But the act of the volunteer transforms the noun into a verb: to volunteer is to offer to do something that you do not have to do, often without having been asked to do it or without expecting payment.

There is selflessness as the conduit to self-knowledge and self-realization both in the act of volunteering and also in the actions taken of a decision to love. Volunteering and love both emerge from the choice to act in service of another's well-being, often without regard to our own immediate interests. The reward of both volunteering and loving is the growth one gets in the aftermath of expressing the kind of vulnerability that can be available in these relationships. Perhaps that is why the love one chooses through friendships can be so particularly transformative: it exists only because of dedication and personal responsibility.

I used to think that being great lay in large gestures and magnified impact. But the thirty years of volunteering to be Steacy's mentor and friend have demonstrated that greatness and magnified impact often lies in the tiniest gestures. Showing up. Calling. Listening. Caring. Being there when things go sideways. Being there, too, when things are great. Wearing the short-shorts that your sister badgers you into buying. Taking the dive off the high board at the swimming pool. Extending the invitation to spend time together. Going on video call when your hair's not right and your under-eyes are baggy. Risking being disliked, telling harsh truths, and making her write it down in a letter to herself. Sharing photos from thirty years ago. Petting the goat when you don't want to. Hugging the sequoia tree. Making the call to say you're sorry. Writing the postcard when you're in Venice. Trying on the high boots. Making the calls and helping to fix the messes they've made when they have committed to doing right. Booking the cabin in the woods. Spending a whole long car ride really trying to learn the difference between Nicki Minaj and Rihanna. Showing up for celebratory moments and making sure you capture the photographs.

I'm blessed by the past thirty years because I've been blessed by the friendship I've volunteered to undertake. We are not impotent in love. Our choices, our volunteering, are powerful. By the act of volunteering, we can change the world and how we show up in it and change ourselves for those we choose to have in our lives.

On Poetry

There is poetry on the New York City Subway system. Literally. From time to time, and usually at the back of cars, instead of ads there are poems. The poems are beautifully rendered and accompanied by artists' illustrations. The program is called "Poetry in Motion," and I consider it to be a gem of the city in plain sight. If the subway is the city's arterial system, this program reminds us that poetry is the city's heartbeat and what keeps it in motion.

Poetry is woven within the fabric of New York City. When I was last in Williamsburg, Brooklyn (a long time ago, now that there's a pandemic going on), I saw poetry etched as graffiti across buildings. One of my favorite streets in Manhattan is on the east side of Midtown, approaching the main doors of the Central Library. Etched into the sidewalk are quotations and other inspiring words, many of which are lifted from poems. Today, poetry flourishes in Brooklyn and Queens, and for a half century, the Bronx has conjured up rap and hip-hop, an urgent blend of poetry and music. Lower Manhattan's history is littered with poetry, and Harlem's renaissances, all of them, are intertwined with the poetry of resistance. I don't know how many streets in the city are doubly named, and how many of them have poets as their secondary designation, but I'd imagine it's more than a trivial amount.

Perhaps poetry has recently re-exploded into our consciousness following the Biden inauguration's inclusion of youth poet laureate Amanda Gormon. Suddenly, there was a poem that crystallized its availability as a thing we can go out and buy and read and consume and recite. People recognized that poetry can be powerful. A good poem will communicate to us and move us. We understand, even imperfectly, that poetry can catalyze the spirit and move us to translate that spirit to action. We start to reach into understanding of why it was poets of the Eastern Bloc, in Hungary and East Germany, who were leading their peoples toward the future as the Iron Curtain fell around them.

This youth poet laureate experienced poetry in school and so had years to begin perfecting her craft. All children have poetry in them, and it is a remarkable development that the writing of poetry should be taught in schools. We have concealed the power of poetry by teaching it only as plays or on the page disembodied from performance, or in forcing students to memorize and recite it by rote. By stripping the activity of creating poetry from the action of consuming it and declaiming it with their voices, we train students to engage with poetry superficially and to overlook its role in becoming who we are, and in building the environments we inhabit.

Poetry is motion, in words merging with imagery. Poetry is the art of compression, of choosing words with sufficient deliberation and care to speed imagery and tone into a snapshot of awareness. Poetry reminds us that we can be too casual with words, that we can forget their meaning and power. Poetry reminds us that we don't really listen to the sound and meaning of what we say. Poetry reminds us that the crystallization of meaning within sound can conjure visions and help us see our world anew with eyes reopened. Poetry translates our relationship with what we understand to be reality. In compression of language, poetry merges us with new ideas, connections, and awareness.

A poem, if you let it, will grab you. Whether it is a few words or many, it will affix images or situations for mediation in the imagination. The best poems are specific and use concrete imagery and words to underscore the relationship of the part to the whole to facilitate integration. Perhaps for this reason, poetry has often been used both as a tool in resistance movements and as a mechanism for indoctrination within an ideology. Neither of these are inherently good nor bad: resistance to a system can be used to fight injustice; it can also be used to destabilize an order that is serving its people well. It is poetry in the speeches of politicians and activists that have moved people to action.

Perhaps, too, because poetry is memorable and often short, it tends to survive stressors such as wars, imprisonment, or gulags. It can be remembered and carried when systems of oppression or calamity make taking longer works impossible. It is poetry that people in mythology carried to the underworld and back. This may also be why postapocalyptic works use the same conceit: it was those that could remember poetry that were the source of hope against the burning of books in *Fahrenheit 451*.

As a child I wrote poetry, and if I had been asked to answer honestly the question of what I wanted to do with my life, it's possible I might have said, "I want to be a poet." I still don't know if poets are called or created, but I do know the forces that work against pursuing poetry as a career. For most, it is unnervingly not economical, at least today in America, unless paired with music. I hope this situation changes and that we awaken to what is available to us when we consume poetry a little more frequently than we do. And I hope, too, that we learn what becomes available to us all when we work to create poetry, when we have to sit down and apply the economy of compression to our words to crystallize our message in an image. In a world of abundance, poetry encourages us to select the words, images, and ideas that we need to keep close or memorize. Poetry trains us to understand, feel, and embody only that which is truly necessary to carry to the other side. Poetry grounds us to the spot and to each other and provides shared vision and community. Poetry is a salve and a pathway to integration with our world and with each other. It is a shared experience around the campfire. It moves us together. Poetry moves us.

Poetry humanizes us in a busy, noisy, reckless world that often disdains us. It rises us up because it is uniquely human; we are not us, as humans, as individuals, without poetry.

On Mourning

We do not always recognize the mourning we do as grief. We often correlate the public acknowledgment of grief to the outward signs of bereavement, such as wearing black armbands or black clothes. We bind grief to the loss of significant loved ones and assign specific rituals to its expression. There is no doubt that the loss of a loved one is traumatic. Or that social cataclysms, including this pandemic, can involve generalized grief and mourning. But we diminish the potential of mourning when we limit it to specific forms of trauma.

All grief marks an emotional injury, and grief can cut deep and leave permanent, though not always visible, scars. Many events can lead to minor mourning, which remains no less necessary to address feelings of bereavement than other circumstances of loss. We can intuitively grasp that mourning is related to big, external loss, whether it is the loss of a loved one or a family pet, the destruction of property, or the loss of a significant relationship. But we can lose other things we hold dear, such as our self-perception, a belief, an understanding, our sense of self as we relate to a character in a book or movie, or our ideas about how things ought to work. All of these situations involve loss: of self-identify, self-esteem, self-regard. The loss of how we understand ourselves to be and of our place in the world can be no less injurious than when we lose our relationship to something fixed, such as a person or a job. Loss of our interior space is still a loss. We need to acknowledge the need to mourn and heal from emotional injuries.

Writers are told we need to be ready to "kill our darlings." In meditation today, I realized I have resisted this maxim when I have not wanted to let go of an imaginative creation. This resistance has time and again proved to be the biggest block to creation that I experience. I have learned that creation involves destruction and, more precisely, grief and the ability to process emotions associated with letting go of ideas or expectations of what a work should have been. Writing is hard because we need the emotional resilience to continue to let go—so too in life.

We think we are one way. Yet time passes and we discover we have new tastes or that our self-identity was an illusion. Friends that were once critical to us fall away. We cease certain activities, or age intervenes in our pursuits, and how we once showed up in the world is no longer either accessible or desirable. How we translate our relationships to ourselves as we change and age may depend on how well we mourn the death of one conception of ourselves and our rebirth into something new. At times we may welcome this transformation. At other times, mourning this loss of self may be difficult, particularly if we feel that the change was forced upon us, because we were not ready and did not choose it. It can be hard to let go, but if we recognize and work through the emotional injury by mourning, we can discover what is newly available to us.

Mourning is never easy when the loss is intangible, but it is available.

Rituals can give shape and form to mourning and can help orient others to our condition and how they can help us move through grief. Mourning requires patience and community support and compassion, and grieving rituals help shape community response. Much like physical injuries involve signals about healing and cues about help the injured party needs, grieving rituals shape public perception and response to healing from emotional injuries. Mourning intangible private injuries can be difficult because there is no set of rituals associated with grieving the loss of well-being or of identity associated with job loss, loss of a skill due to aging, or loss of self-regard when one comes to realize "I'm no longer the person I thought I was." For many, any healing rituals in these situations are inchoate, personal, and possibly not understood by others.

No wonder so much mourning turns up as anxiety, mild depression, or lassitude. We do not have rituals to help us through many forms of mourning, and so we can languish, neither letting go of what caused in the injury nor moving along into the new and into healing.

Over the years I have had to contend with grieving the loss of who I thought I was. For so long, I lacked the understanding that I was grieving and simply couldn't be patient with resistance to letting go of objects or purging the names and numbers of people out of my contacts list. I languish and procrastinate when I can't process grief; often I also experience a moderate dose of anxiety for good measure. Yet I have come to almost delight in situations where I recognize the tug of an emotional injury, because that also means that something is falling away, and I have an opening to be something different. Now I am starting to recognize such feelings as a sign of growth.

Our physical injuries, even while painful and debilitating, can bring us awareness of our body's miraculous ability to heal. Similarly, our emotional injuries showcase our remarkable ability to transform, learn, and grow.

Translating these private journeys of grief into a public language of mourning can facilitate traversing the chasm of loss, even over something trivial. I have taken to writing what I am mourning on tape that I stick to the bottom of my running shoes. That way I not only literally run a distance over what I am mourning, but I can metaphorically put it underfoot and understand myself to be carrying myself over it. I have learned to give away objects into which I have invested emotional energy, to literally clear space for new things and their energy. I take time to review social media contacts and phone contacts and clear out names I don't intentionally connect with. As I get older, I understand it is important to proactively embrace mourning and that resisting it will keep me stuck.

Mourning is never easy, and it is not supposed to be, but it is necessary and healthful. Emotional injuries can leave scars and, much like physical injuries to the body if not fully healed, can leave us fearful to move, less flexible, and more prone to future injury. To keep the spirit resilient and emotional health in balance, we must all learn to mourn the intangible, to take the time and space necessary to acknowledge the wound, and to implement the rituals that we need to let the light and healing in.

Especially now, over one year into a socially scarring pandemic, we need to mourn intangible losses alongside our actual dead. We need to mourn dreams that were shattered, livelihoods that were transformed, and relationships that were translated during a year in quarantine. We will take stock of who we were during our time in quarantine and whether that accorded, or not, with our self-regard. How did we fare? What do we need to discard? Who did we become, and what path are we on to becoming?

In death, even a metaphorical one, there is rebirth, but only if we let go, only if we mourn. Grief is a gift, even if it is an unwelcome one. Grief shows up as an uninvited guest and can stalk us silently until the moment we realize it has left the party, and we acknowledge the opportunity in the space it's left behind in our hearts and right in front of our eyes.

On Stillness

The quality of stillness can be like a deep, calm pool: we admire its beauty but might panic if plunged unexpectedly headlong into it. We imagine the tranquility and calm of stillness but often resist immersing ourselves into such a state. We panic, avoid, and numb out rather than surrender to stillness. Why?

The quietness, inactivity, silence, and lack of movement involved in stillness can be experienced as opposite to our usual state of being and can feel uncomfortable. Too often our first instinct tells us to do something when confronted with discomfort, to add to the situation rather than to subtract. Stillness can feel like a dark cavern of inactivity that we must either fill up or avoid. The narrative of our culture is one of doing things, being things, or having things, all of which are about activity and activation. Ours is a culture of being seen and being heard, of leaving a mark, of making an impact, and being out in the world.

Stillness doesn't fit within that narrative. Stillness is not about being out in the world, but about receiving the world and surrendering to it. That posture can feel like a loss, but only in that the activity of our doing is removed. We can be made to feel deeply uncomfortable by this perception of lack of control. Or rather, what can make us feel uncomfortable is the reminder that all too often things really are unpredictable. For many, the sheer randomness, unpredictability, and savagery of fate is scary, a thought we want to avoid.

Stillness is a subtraction, but it is not nothing. It involves a conscious choice to quiet, to surrender, to perceive, to receive. Stillness is not a passive state. The quality of stillness nudges us to remain open, to see what arises, and to perceive what is available to be perceived. We quiet our expectations and our preconceptions.

Stillness highlights the distinction between willpower and being willing. With willpower, we push; with willingness, we are open to receive. Our discomfort with stillness can show us the gap between our self-perception of openness and our capacity to receive. It can feel uncomfortable to have our ideas shift or to have our certainty revealed as illusion.

Too often we think we know the way the world is, but our understanding of the world is often only what we want to see. We don't actually perceive the world as it is. Perception and reception are related. To see what is actually there requires us to be willing to receive what is available to be perceived. In stillness, we stop and let the world in.

It can be scary to let the world in. It's a state of vulnerability that can feel like boundaries dissolving. It can feel like a loss of control or a loss of the self. We fear being hurt, injured, or having our weaknesses exposed. Vulnerability, like stillness, is about perception and seeing things as they are. That capacity for being hurt or injured was always there; in vulnerability we acknowledge it.

Vulnerability also highlights the distinction between willpower and willingness. With willpower, we avoid or ignore what can injure us, including emotionally. When we are vulnerable, we know how we can be hurt but act anyway. We are open to the possibility that we could be hurt and the equal possibility that we might not be hurt. We don't actually know what might happen in the future, but we don't let the past dictate choices and are open to receiving what unfolds. Vulnerability is the dimension of stillness that enables connection because it facilitates the willingness to perceive and receive another person or a situation without illusion. When we say someone loves us for who we really are, we are acknowledging this state of vulnerability.

Vulnerability is not weakness; it's clarity. It reveals what is, what we can and cannot control, and from there we can channel right-action. We quiet the action of working against what we cannot change so that we direct our energy into what we can change. As we become clearer about what is ours to do, we distinguish our illusions about the world, about others, about our self-perception, and about our relationships to others. Paradoxically, vulnerability can help us get very clear about what is ours and what is theirs.

Vulnerability also highlights our fundamental state of interconnectedness. Too often what hurts us, what makes us injured or uncomfortable, and the things that don't suit us are structural or are transpersonal in the sense that what we feel is actually transmitted among people. We are feeling a cultural malaise rather than an individual one. Putting pressure on individuals to change what is beyond any one person to change can lead to hopelessness and burnout expressed as numbing or avoidance. The antidote may be cultivating moments in which we experience a state of stillness. Stillness will open us up and increase vulnerability, and it may help us define the boundaries that refine our understanding of what we can truly control.

We are all swimming in the dark, still waters of life. When we are plunged into water over our heads and fear drowning, we can grasp furiously, lash out, and panic. In water, these sharp, erratic movements can be counterproductive and increase the risk of drowning, which we think of as death, but it's not. Drowning is a process, one devoid of stillness. First there is struggle, often in silence, and agitation before submersion when the head sinks below the surface. Then the drowning victim holds their breath, which can lead to excruciating pain. The body experiences a lack of oxygen and an increase in carbon dioxide, and the patterns needed for health are reversed. The body needs oxygen and will eventually trigger a breath automatically; underwater, water is inhaled. Even if the larynx closes, the victim will become unconscious. The spasm ends, and water fills the lungs, often causing them to collapse. When breathing ceases, the heart may continue to beat, but will work harder, which may lead to a cardiac event. Eventually the heart will stop.

We can drown in water, but we can also drown in emotions or in our illusions of how we perceive things to be. Like the water, the flow of life and time cannot be grasped, and it does not help to struggle against it. If we can arrest the struggle, we can prevent our heads from going under the surface of illusion. If we can continue to still ourselves and remain open and vulnerable, we can prevent our hearts stopping for a little while longer.

On Presence

For Stuart C.

We are encouraged to seize the day. To be mindful. To be present in the moment. These aphorisms have one thing in common: they place attention on our own awareness of being in the *now*. Particularly over this pandemic year when so much has felt constricting and uncertain, we have been encouraged to abate fear and isolation with meditation, by centering on our breath, focusing on what we can control, and not letting our regrets of the past or our thoughts of the future interfere with the here and now. It's true that drawing mindshare into what is before us can help reduce anxiety and channel our energy and actions when situations feel overwhelming. Too many thoughts about the future, which is inherently uncertain, can tend toward anxiety, fear, and self-doubt. Lingering too long on the past can induce feelings of nostalgia, depression, and regret. Getting stuck with these feelings can drain energy from right-action and doing what needs to be done next. We can also place too much weight on circumstances that are not involved in what is before us, distorting our perceptions. These aphoristic reminders to be present to ourselves and the moment can be restorative, particularly if we observe that our current actions and awareness are not aligned with what we claim we most value. They can be good at checking self-intention.

I often ground myself while running, whether alone or in a group. I find that the rhythm of running, coupled with the need to breathe deeply, helps me relax. Running gets me out of my head and puts my problems into perspective. I can be having what I think of as a bad day but will go for a run and almost always—probably because I put my problems to the side for that time—come back with a different perspective. Perhaps because it keeps my attention focused only on what is before me, running can help me brainstorm ideas, put things in perspective, and separate what I can't control from what I can. Running encourages me to understand my own strengths and weaknesses. I find running liberating and self-affirming: I see what I can do and the results of my own efforts.

But what if individual attentiveness and self-awareness is not the most critical aspect of being present? What if presence isn't only about our own state but how we show up for others? What would happen if we shifted our perspective and focused our attention on who we are in the eyes of others and how we show up for them?

By this, I do not mean that we would be better off if we considered how we would be judged by others. Too often, thinking about how others will judge us induces fear because we can't control what others think. How others judge us is usually superficial and may involve another's subjective and solipsistic criteria that reflect more about the judger's insecurities and beliefs than they do about the person being judged. Judgment is almost always about the self, even when it purports to be directed at others. So often what irks us in others and what we judge about them is our own faults as we imagine them reflected back at us.

This may be why focus on how we show up in others' lives can be an uplifting practice. If our presence permits others to grow and shine, to accomplish their dreams, to enlarge their own capacity, aren't we also uplifted? When we show up for another so that they may conquer fear, show them love or compassion, allow them to showcase their generosity or knowledge, or help them achieve something they dream of, aren't we presently living into a better moment, even if that moment isn't about us?

It surprises non-runners to learn that running is a team sport, but any runner who runs with a group, or even with another run partner, understands this. Often, a runner new to group running experiences noticeable gains in speed and strength almost immediately. Why is this? Runners are stronger together. We learn and test our limits, get encouragement, and hold paces we did not think were possible for longer. Many runners will tell you the most intimate conversations they have occur on a long run, when strides matched without eye contact can loosen the tongue. Even in the quiet foot strikes of a long run undertaken without talking, the camaraderie makes us feel both less alone and less crazy.

Even when a group runner runs alone, the memory of the group and the potential of the next group run may imprint itself. When I run alone, the thought in the back of my mind is that I need to keep the consistency up, to keep up my strength when I return to the group. Sometimes we want to ensure we don't fall behind the pack, so that we won't be judged by others. But mostly we want to hold up our end of the group bargain and want to be there for other members of the group as they are there for us when we are feeling low, tired, or flagging.

I learned from running that feelings and emotions are intrapersonal, in that they are infectious and spread within a group. A feeling of weakness or tiredness can be overcome by tapping into the strength within a group. A group can also inspire positivity and optimism. We show up for others we care about to add our intentions to the collective. These intentions and feelings are transmitted, unintentionally sometimes, but at other times deliberately with volition. A group can pull out the best in us if we are open to receive it and when our intention is to bring our best selves to the group.

The head coach of our run group organized an impromptu track meet of two races: 800m and 400m. As an aging runner who hasn't trained for those distances in decades, I had no business racing. And yet, early on a Saturday morning, on a public, vaguely tended, rubberized track, I launched myself headlong into both these events, determined to try and to be open to the experience and just see what happened. There was, for me, a real risk of injury, and possibly of embarrassment. But no matter.

I decided that showing up and lending my presence to the effort of the group, by being there to acknowledge and intentionally build my coach's dream, was valuable. I understood that the contribution of my effort to the whole was cumulatively more important than any specific time I ran. That to show up and throw weight into the potential of a track meet in the city, in a pandemic, was something we all needed. That to show up to help someone else achieve a dream was the best, most productive, most self-actualized expression of being available in that moment. That the priority of my presence there was a contribution most aligned with how it was possible for me to show up.

And you know what? I had fun. I ran a couple of good races, though perhaps not with the results I wanted or what might be possible if I applied myself to those distances. And I am reminded that presence is always a two-way gift, with the giver receiving blessings too. Now I dream within a larger dream of possibility what we, I, us, may all become and achieve. We are all stronger and better for having shown up.

We need to stay grounded in our present, yes: but when we show up for others in a right-sized way that enlarges possibility, we are all winners. If half of winning is showing up, we see that our presence can enlarge opportunity in ways we may not always imagine for others, and that may take us beyond limits we had not even understood as our invisible edges.

On Abundance

New York City is starting to reopen after this pandemic year of restriction, isolation, and uncertainty. I've just passed Lincoln Center on a walk. A great structure is erected in the courtyard there: it's a new city park with artificial turf and benches. This will soon become an outdoor concert venue, but for now it has become a gathering place mobbed with playful children and weary, wary parents. Laughter and shrieks of delight soar up to the sky. Cars, yellow cabs, trucks, and buses adorn the roadways again, and the hum of traffic resumes as Manhattan's soundtrack. The subways are filling up, restoring their ridership, a riot of personalities, styles, and stories.

What has always struck me about what makes New York City great is its absurdity of abundance. The city seethes and beats; it teems. It is a crush of people, a swarm of rats and roaches, a complex of dreams. New York is architecture haphazard, a network of bodegas serving neighborhoods as distinct and varied as the fashion and hairstyles dotting the streets. New York is every language, every food and spice, every profession, and every heartbreak. It is a bottomless cup, an eternal buffet of emotion, intrigue, and synchronicity. The pandemic suspended this abundance.

During the pandemic time, many of us retreated indoors into sensory deprivation chambers. Some of us did not have unmediated contact with others. Others were forced out into situations in which no one could be trusted. We were separated from family, friends, activities, work, and the beat of the city. Anxiety, depression, ennui, boredom, and languishing followed.

Crisis followed: personal, intrapersonal, and societal. People lost work, relationships, lovers, and loved ones. Crime went up. Stores shuttered. Hunger increased. Parts of the city emptied out. Dislocation, depression, and desperation haunted us, even if not directly. It often seemed like a dark cloud hung overhead, even on a bright sunny day.

During the past long year, some suggested a coping strategy to manage negative emotions might be to focus on gratitude. Gratitude is the state of being thankful. Certainly, it is helpful to pay attention to what you have rather than what you lack and to anchor each day in appreciation. Gratitude and thankfulness can be an antidote to materialist culture or a perceived set of personal or situational deficiencies. It is believed that gratitude can help foster a positive rather than a negative mindset and may help focus attention away from fear and anxiety toward being present in the moment. A practice of gratitude may enlarge the view away from what one can't do or have toward what one *can* do or have. And because the pandemic removed so many people, habits, and practices—and in some cases vocations and avocations—from our lives, focusing on the good that remained may have served to remind us of what wasn't lost.

But instead of gratitude, I discovered that I focused on abundance. This shift from gratitude to abundance brought me the world. Gratitude and abundance are related but distinct. Abundance is the condition of being in rich supply, of having a plentiful amount. What I discovered over the past year was that abundance just *is*, whether it relates to me or not; that abundance, in itself, can be celebrated. In the darkest days of the pandemic, when I took time to recall what made me most thankful, I uncovered abundance, and it was everywhere. Even as I endured an unending scream of ambulance sirens while on an evening stroll to the Jackie O. Reservoir, my route took me under an abundance of budding cherry trees, blossoms everywhere. If I was prepared to stop and listen, I heard an abundance of birds. And everywhere was evidence of an abundance of kindness and respect for others. While many fled, those who remained banged pots and pans every night.

In those evenings when it was most difficult to cope, I would settle down on a mat on my floor and just breathe: an abundance of air would fill my lungs, and I'd count to four before exhaling. I had an abundance of air, yet so many didn't have even that.

Sometimes I would recognize that the abundance I had was rooted in gratitude, but often something else, either joy or fear or sadness. A focus on abundance kept me connected to all my emotions as they arose and passed. The ability to feel and process an abundance of emotions may be the critical prerequisite to a richer, more comprehensive mental health. We need to experience and process feelings in their variety, and gratitude helps us process emotions in their variety—we can be thankful that we have the opportunity to feel so many emotions. Abundance may be the world's default state, even if every individual does not experience the world that way. We can feel a lack, and the world can still be abundant.

I discovered that rejoicing in the world's abundance in its availability and possibility transcended and transformed my relationship to everything. Gratitude situates me in thankfulness for what has occurred in the past that I experience now. Abundance lets me see that what is here now may continue into the future. It sits beyond things that can be had or experienced into what just is. It is less about having and more about being.

As I get older, I find my greater joys come often from abundance: of love, happiness, community, experience, food, birds, children's laughter, cars on the streets, and also of people returning, of quiet time, of potential, of hope.

When we see and experience our abundance, we realize the richness available to us. An abundance of friends, thinking of me and wishing me well, reminds me I have community. An abundance of potential of what might be, whether positive or negative, in the future, simply because I am still here, binds me to life. An abundance of beauty and serenity, because I pass so many tulips on a walk in the park, roots me in time. I wonder at how small we are, and yet how infinite we are as a part of a greater whole.

As New York City starts to reopen, as we move uncertainly, boldly, and with fear and enthusiasm toward what comes next, I welcome back the expressions of its abundance, the city's shear madness, proliferation, and beauty. I smile as I cross Amsterdam Avenue and hear the sound of children's laughter bouncing off the buildings in Lincoln Center.

On Time

What distinguishes a life is time: how time is understood, perceived, mediated, and used. Time is our birthright, although we are each granted it in different measures and the experienced quality of it may vary within and between lives. While I have always understood this, it's taken me decades to appreciate in my bones the salience of time, how valuable and fragile it is, and yet how rich. Life is time, and time is life.

I have not always understood how time operates within my life, and I have not been good at perceiving and mediating time. By this I mean that I have respected time's place in my life, but I have not always been considerate of my place in time.

I have respected time's place in my life by being punctual. I have set my watches and clocks correctly. I am rarely late and usually meet deadlines. I have respected time by observing the structures of a day and the patterns of seasons. I have adjusted to daily rhythms, developed routines, schedules, and habits. I have tried to grow old gracefully, conscious of how time changes experiences and societal expectations. I thought that in doing all this I had mastered a relationship with time because I respected time's place in my life: I treated time as a static element to be negotiated, the way one would relate to or manage a thing or event.

But not so: it is also important to make room for and respect one's place in time, because time is a flow. We are within time constantly, rather than outside it or periodically related to it. Time doesn't stop because we don't think about it. Time doesn't depend on our clocks or the seasons; those things merely serve to highlight its passage. Time is a process, and mastery of time is impossible. Time is only a dynamic relationship; it is only an unfolding of being.

I have become convinced that thinking of the self as outside the flow of time leads to confusion and suffering, sometimes even emotional and physical pain. Our relationship to time and how we mediate being in its flow may be a primary marker of our health and well-being. Our physical health surely reveals this, simply because the body degrades with time. More saliently, lifestyle illnesses can only develop over time. I have long believed that how I live today will impact how I feel later. We know that eating and sleeping poorly contributes to feeling lousy the next day and can increase stress and irritation. How I eat, sleep, and exercise today will show up in how I feel in ten years. We know the healthy habits add up, both immediately and over time.

But the same may be true emotionally. Too often I have tried to live parts of my life outside time, struggling against it. I catch myself casting backward and revisiting the past with nostalgia or regret. I may rework conversations or situations in my head, wishing or wanting them to be different, usually arising from some desire for things to be better or for myself to be better. Or thinking of the past conjures up some victory or hurt that I reexperience again, often to avoid feeling something now. At other times, I am thinking into the future and its inherent uncertainty. I can become paralyzed by decisions and overanalyze what might occur. My anxiety and irritation will rise, and I'll experience stress even though nothing has happened. Or I'll become engrossed in fantasy and use this to buoy my spirits, which is a different and easier vector of contentment than achievement.

While it's enjoyable to periodically revisit happy memories or dream into the potential of the future, becoming detached from the present flow of time disrupts our emotional state and perceptions of well-being. Casting about too long in the future without crystalizing those aspirations into actions now, or lingering over past behavior without celebrating or letting go of it removes one from perceiving right-action in the present moment. Being able to return to where we are in the flow of time and transfer those inputs into current thoughts, behaviors, and actions ensures we stay properly grounded. We can't necessarily do anything about what happened in the past, but we can accept it and learn from it. We can recast our errors and hurts as lessons. We can fear the future or hope into it, or we can take steps to prepare for it with actions now. After all, how we feed our bodies and our emotional selves now is how we will show up in ten years. Or tomorrow.

Getting right-sized and present into time may also contribute to our using what time we have in a way that is consistent with our actual desires and possibilities.

Spending time outside the flow, either wallowing in the past or fearing or dreaming about the future, indulges escapist activities. Time will continue to flow without our intervention, and being outside of time results in time perhaps spent without any growth. We may never feel enriched by how that time was expended.

But why do we do this? Why do we not respect time and procrastinate, divert our attention away from awareness of the now, live in the past and not let go, not act on our dreams, eat poorly, or get distracted? Why can this be so hard?

I don't know, except that I think it's about fear of uncertainty and insecurity, and it's easier to live feeling like one has mastery over moments of time, fantasizing that we are controlling the clock rather than getting to live within the flow of time. To know constantly that one is within time is to always live with the awareness that time will continue long after what's a "you" has ceased to be. That's hard to confront; it's both abstract and immediate, precise and uncertain. It requires one to get up close to death and acknowledge its eventuality. But it's necessary and certain that one day our time will end, whether or not we live out our time with this awareness.

Earlier this week I took a long walk through the woods in a national park without any other humans around. I walked up a small mountain and along a trail to a pond near the summit. Part of the mountain has been transformed to pasture, but much of it remained covered in trees. The trail crossed various creeks that took water out of the pond to a river that flowed to the base of the mountain.

When I am in nature, I connect with environments much larger than me, including that of time. In a forest, if we care to look, we see everywhere the processes of decay, erosion, petrification, and new growth. We see the passage of time in the cycles of nature, and can place individuals—whether they are trees, flowers, birds, insects, or animals—within that cycle. We, too, are in that cycle, though we have become skilled at maintaining the illusion that we are removed from it.

Perhaps we find comfort, relaxation, and peace in nature in part because it reminds us of our place in time, rather than time's place in our lives, and this peace reflects our sense of connection. Part of our well-being depends on connection to a larger whole. In nature, we can be released from our watches into the rhythm of the sun and the flow of water and wind. We can slow down and remind ourselves that life happens one moment at a time, within a series of thousands of interlocked moments. It may be that we live life to the fullest when our experience of time is identical to its passage. Paradoxically, living in the present mediates time completely. Nature reveals that as much as flow degrades and dissolves, it also transmutes and petrifies—strengthening and rendering permanent its objects—and so, too, we can become like trees petrified by water if we allow ourselves to be in the right place at the right time.

On Solitude

As New York City moves through the agita, hurly-burly, and delight of reopening, I've secreted myself off to an undisclosed rural location for a spot of solitude. It's a long weekend, and despite having time and access to a car where I'm staying, I've decided to stay put in a cabin by myself. I have food, a book or two, and a view that overlooks a grassy field, a forest, and a mountain. My plan is to sit with my thoughts and decompress. When I return to the city, it's back to work for me, with its commute, crowds, and social contact. I suppose that I am taking this time to mentally prepare for the what-next, even if it's a return to a pattern I've followed for thirty or so years, this gap year notwithstanding.

The irony is that the solitude I have here is, practically speaking, no different from the solitude I've just experienced over the past year with its period of lockdown and work from home. Since I live alone, I've had ample solitude. For almost three months last year, at the onset of the pandemic and the first shelter-in-place order, I only went outside at unusual times of day and retreated from people. I had over one hundred days of uninterrupted aloneness and many more days alone over the past fifteen months.

Solitude is a state of seclusion that can have both positive and negative effects. Much of the how we experience solitude depends on context. Solitude can be a time to be alone, and short-term solitude can be revitalizing, particularly where it provides a time to relax, or reconnect with parts of self, or to work, think, and rest without interruption. Many people value a period of solitude for the privacy.

But solitude can also arise from isolation, and since humans are fundamentally social creatures, that kind of solitude can also have negative effects, including boredom, lethargy, irritability, and anxiety. Long periods of isolation can lead to distortions of time and perception, clinical depression, or an impairment of relationships. Language reveals how to distinguish between the positive and negative effects of solitude: *alone* denotes time with only oneself experienced positively, and *loneliness* refers to the negative experience of isolation. *Alone* refers to the times we desire to be without people, while *lonely* refers to the times we desire human contact and connection. Loneliness is an emotion in which someone feels pain by a perceived lack of intimacy with others (or themselves). Loneliness occurs when someone wants sympathy or companionship but does not get it.

Our experience of solitude depends on our perception of it. If we think the solitude is awful, it is. Although our society uses solitude (solitary confinement, scapegoating, and exile) as a form of punishment, we also use solitude as a form of meditation, as a means to achieve spiritual enlightenment, as a mechanism for grieving, and as a refuge.

The solitude I have now is a welcome respite that delivers an opportunity to reset and recharge, to gather together my energy and inner resources, and to ensure my inner compass is aligned with my intended direction of travel. This solitude is beneficial because I intend for it to be experienced that way.

The solitude so many people experienced during the lockdowns of the pandemic was understood differently. There were times when I experienced the isolation of the pandemic as a burden; I was alone, afraid, and lonely. It was hard to get information and comfort. The endless days blended together, leaving me disorientated, bored, restless, and anxious. I was sometimes beset by a feeling that time was slipping by, and that I should be doing something—but what? Such thoughts increased feelings of malaise and despondency, particularly when I was awakened at night or overheard the wailing sirens of ambulances outside at indeterminate distances.

I wanted to travel but felt boxed in; I wanted to see people, but they were inaccessible; I wanted to have human contact and touch, but this activity brought forth risk and social opprobrium. I was atomized within my bubble of one.

But I also lived aspects of my best life in those months of the pandemic. The nature, character, and content of my relationships with others changed. Some relationships that existed only due to habit and proximity faded away. Things I did, people I saw, and meetings I attended out of habit or duty were interrupted, giving me an opportunity to reset priorities and terminate practices that no longer provided value, contentment, or connection. Friendships of long duration, especially those I rarely saw in person, had the opportunity to expand and become refreshed if we chose to establish new patterns through calls, texts, or videoconferencing. Freed from commuting time, I developed and practiced new routines that have nurtured strength and creativity.

But most importantly, perhaps, is the self-connection that's been revitalized. Without others to distract me, I have rediscovered joy and space in my own company. So much time alone concentrates the attention if we are lucky, and I was lucky. At first, I started and abandoned so many should-dos before realizing the opportunity before me was in subtraction. That the privacy and peace I could discover only in my own company would emerge from simplicity. That doing fewer things, not more, would provide greater inner spiritual nourishment because I was generating more opportunities to connect with those activities and things I was doing.

This connection reduced my sense of loneliness and anxiety because I was more deliberate about how I spent my time and energy. I learned that the value of solitude occurs when one takes a greater measure of one's internal space. I discovered I really did contain multitudes, and I experienced a greater range of emotions than was previously available to me, rendering life as fuller. Too often, my previous inability to connect to an emotion, to find its location within my internal space, had caused me to isolate or shun it. Inherently, I was not connecting with some part of myself, and this lack of integration could generate the residual effects associated with loneliness: lethargy, irritability, anxiety, or in times of acute lack of self-connection, depression.

The pandemic served up for me a spiritual retreat I hadn't planned for and didn't know I needed. The gift I received from the solitude was a more complete sense of wholeness. It's not that I've achieved peace, enlightenment, or bliss. Instead, it's that I can recognize that these states can be available to me because they are emotions that can be felt and experienced if I slow down to feel them. Perhaps I need this weekend away, in solitude, to have a final practice round of emotional integration before heading back into the reopened New York City, where the pressures on a person can lead them to dissociate, to separate within and without, as a means to attempt to control the chaos and unpredictability.

And I have learned this lesson: so much of what occurs to us is unpredictable, but we have control over how we respond. We can curb an experience of loneliness by finding spaces within to connect to; we can adjust how we frame other experiences to tie them to our resilience.

When I first arrived in this isolated rural spot, it was late. I was alone in the quiet, and the sun was setting. I stepped outside to take two photographs minutes apart: during the time the sun went down and when its light went out. Darkness can be an emptiness, a source of fear and foreboding. But then the stars came out, or rather, my eyes adjusted, and I could see thousands of points of light. I kept my camera in my pocket as I looked way up, first at the North Star, then past the Milky Way and into the vastness of space and imagined what it contains, what could be next.

On Growth

I received a packet of unlabeled mystery seeds after attending an event in Central Park, and I don't know what they will grow into, whether flowers or herbs. When it was warm enough in Manhattan for me to plant them, I put them in a pot that I watered and placed in the sun. I wasn't sure what, if anything, would happen to them.

Every morning, I peek to see how much progress has occurred in that plant pot. The growth is not perceptible day to day but is apparent over time. Tracking the cumulative progress of these little plants brings me great joy, and I delight in wonder. Less than two months ago there wasn't even fresh dirt in this pot, let alone these green shoots. These plants and the seeds from which they come are amazing. I am not a gardener and never have been, but I have always enjoyed being surrounded by greenery, and it's only now that I am in a city largely devoid of green that I have had to take matters into my own hands and create my own plant oasis. But the plants in this pot reveal my inexperience: I didn't know how to space them out; I still don't know whether or how much to prune them. Although I give them water and ensure they have sun, these little stalks are really on their own. I have much to learn here, but I am paying attention.

As I've watched these shoots get bigger, I've meditated more generally on growth, human and societal. Growth is the progressive development of a living thing, characterized by its increasing in size or number. But there is a qualitative meaning too: growth is also about evolution. To grow involves full development: to move from a simple to a complex life-form. In humans this sense of growth means maturity, usually physically but also emotionally and psychologically. We also speak about the growth of societies and the evolution of civilizations in the same way.

Our culture has developed so many celebrations associated with puberty, physical maturity, and the physical life cycle, but we have fewer milestones associated with emotional and psychological growth. Physical maturity is understood to be visible and objective, and we often place so much pressure or anxiety on younger humans to grow up and assume their adult physical forms. In our culture, we often obsess over it.

But no less important to human well-being are other dimensions of development, such as the emotional and psychological. And along these dimensions we grow and evolve; we can get bigger and more numerous in the range and experience of our emotional expression and sense of wholeness. Yet these dimensions of human development are often under-discussed, under-taught, and under-monitored. Our culture does not have an articulated development pathway to measure emotional or psychological evolution. Consequently, we may not know how we are doing, relatively speaking, either individually or collectively. Too often, our physical selves have literally out-developed our other dimensions.

This arresting of any form of growth, including the emotional, can have consequences. Underdeveloped humans can have immature emotional postures by externalizing pain, avoiding, or not processing emotions. More generally, many people are not taught to distinguish or name emotions, even powerful ones, leaving them with a diminished range of words to articulate and metabolize inner worlds. Much like a child needs help navigating the physical world, emotionally immature people may continue to need this assistance but may not realize it. And too often, due to their physical maturity, they are off doing adult things, such as working, marrying, and having kids of their own, but they may not be fully equipped to handle the emotional complexities that life casts at them. Such emotionally underdeveloped people may burden others, especially their families, spouses, or children. In more extreme cases, they become collective problems to resolve.

Something similar occurs with psychological well-being. A lack of integration of experience, whether due to trauma, emotional underdevelopment, or no support, can lead to a fragmentation of the self. I've started to understand low or excessive self-esteem as reflecting a lack of full maturation and development. A mature self knows they are complete as they are, both with gracious and ungracious dimensions: we are all angels and monsters, joyful and rageful, compassionate and selfish, helpful and harmful. It's how to integrate these dimensions and how we choose our expression of them in a manner that is grounded in reality that characterizes our development.

As I've watched this pot and observed these seeds growing, New York City has been opening up from a year of lockdown. People wander about without masks while walking dogs or pushing strollers. A new restaurant opens across the street. The sound of traffic returns, eternally penetrative. The city gets louder and busier. People return to the subways and buses. Groups gather in the park, on sidewalks, and in bars, and people visit the movie houses and theaters. There are hugs and tears and laughter. This increase in the size and abundance of bodies outside, and in our public and familiar spaces, feels like growth. It's easy to celebrate and rejoice in this development.

But this activity also reveals malignant growth and showcases the wounds and scars of the experience of this past year. So much was devastated: businesses closed, street repairs incomplete, people separated, and relationships and families under strain. On my walks I see more begging, more lives reduced to bundles of goods in shopping trolleys, people sitting with an outstretched hand or a head hung low. We remain a dislocated society: some parts growing well, other parts physically, emotionally, and psychologically stunted.

Much like how emotional and psychological maturity require contact with all aspects of self to permit processing and integration, a true economic and social recovery will involve taking a look at these breakdowns and their scars, and naming and processing them. Then we must do the work required to integrate them, to incorporate them into the whole. There is much to celebrate in the reopening of our cities and worlds after the pandemic, but growth occurs across many dimensions. We ignore the most difficult ones to measure, such our society's emotional and psychological resilience after trauma, at a fundamental risk to our collective growth and well-being.

On Undoing

The journey of writing these essays has been the thing that's kept me going emotionally and spiritually this pandemic year. As I come to the numerical limit of what I set out to do, I reflect that what this project reveals, as so many undertakings do, is that it's the process of getting there that is more enriching than arriving at the destination. The experience of life resides in the journey.

These essays have been a great blessing and salve for me. I started writing them as a way of healing from the isolation I was experiencing during the pandemic's first lockdown while living in a small apartment in New York City, to serve as a distraction from the tension and violence that had started to grip the city as the heat started to rise and economic and racial tensions flared following the killing of George Floyd. I had been unnerved from navigating the trifecta that engulfed the year 2020: fear, uncertainty, and doubt. I was overworked, overstressed, and under-stimulated. I had also just celebrated my birthday all alone, and I was sad. I started writing these essays to cheer myself up.

By initially posting these essays on private social media, I reestablished and maintained connection with my community when I could not visit in person; the topics I've written about have become what we exchange notes about during this period of diminished social gatherings. The weekly cadence of publishing them has brought structure to my days. Selecting and contemplating the weekly theme has given a productive direction to my thoughts. The process of writing has brought time together into a weekly rhythm.

Writing these essays became an act of perseverance and discipline, of creativity and commitment. There were many times I delayed and despaired of finding a topic or resisted writing due to fatigue or overwhelm. In some of these times, my feelings themselves became the fuel for, and the topic of, the writing, as the weeks I wrote about exhaustion, overwhelm, and procrastination illustrate.

As I've approached the milestone of this fiftieth essay, my relationship to them has shifted. I have been putting pressure on myself to write the biggest and best essays yet, to go out with a fanfare, to gather up every last iota of creativity I have to deliver and delight. This pressure has only served to paralyze me and block the writing, and there have been days when I've transferred *write essay* from one line on my daily to-do list to the same line the next day. I'm writing today's entry having called in self-forgiveness, reminding myself that perfectionism is toxic, and that these were always only intended to be gifts—of distraction, caring, awe, or interest—for any who decided to read them. It was never for me to determine how any reader would receive or use them.

These enactments of self-forgiveness, grace, and generosity have also revealed the undoing—including my undoing—that has unfolded during this yearlong project.

This project has undone me, broken me down, and laid bare so many of my assumptions, fears, self-doubts, and vulnerabilities that I will never be the same person ever again. The person I thought I am has cracked just a little and, in the light that has been let in, I see I am a different person in the world than I thought I was before this all started.

It is often on the journey that we are reflected back to ourselves differently than who we imagined ourselves to be.

I have always considered myself expansive and imaginative. I have solved tough problems in my professional life and thought I exhibited similar tenacity in my personal life too. But the effort involved in writing these essays over this year has showed me I had underestimated my capabilities. The process has revealed blind spots in my thinking and self-perception. I had always thought I didn't write because I didn't have time, and I was putting it off until retirement or "one day, when I had time." I see now I was engaging in black-and-white thinking: to write a book would take a blank canvas of time, an unending stretch of days with no other commitments. I languished for years wishing I had the time to write without recognizing or taking responsibility for imagining I needed more time than I was prepared, in that moment, to give it. This year has been revelatory in demonstrating that by taking only a few hours a week I can arrive at a body of work if I break that work down and commit the time to do it. My self-induced writer's block—created by my perfectionism—has been utterly undone. Any big project will be accomplished only in pieces: by breaking down the task to its units, and sometimes its smallest ones, or by dividing the matter up among many people or many weeks. Many hands make light work. Many weeks of essays make a pile the size of a book.

The journey begins, after a commitment to proceed, with a single step.

What has also come undone is a residual doubt that I'd have something sustaining to say. Over the years, my confidence has ricocheted between doubt that I have any- thing meaningful to communicate and an abiding faith that people would read what I would write if only I could figure out what the message was that I needed my words to carry. It turns out, these are not either-or propositions: they relate to and fuel each other. A writer must write; a reader may read. A writer needs a reader, like a reader needs a writer, but these two are not opposites: they are orthogonal; they intersect. Writing is a venture, and it is adventure. Writing as an activity is dangerous. To write, and to try to write well, is to travel into the unknown, to risk being lost, shamed, confused, burgled, ignored, for- gotten, or misunderstood.

A writer cannot find the audience without venturing out.

These discoveries of the journey have been my un- doing. One perception of myself has cracked open and exposed another. I have had to let go of an understanding of myself as a blocked writer and a busy professional. I realize I was using my perceived lack of time as an ex- cuse to not do the work, when it was always my choice in what I did and how I perceived myself in time that was the barren fruit. What was blocking me finding my voice was not any lack of writing, but a lack of sharing that writing. What has unfolded is inevitable when one foot is placed repeatedly in front of the other: motion and velocity, volume and mass.

Time, through energy and intention, has materialized in this work. The impact of this writing year on me is more than just the material of these essays. I have reshaped my environment around it. Years of diaries and writing that I've stored in bankers' boxes are now out in my bookshelves. I've taken to carrying notebooks and jotting observations and snatched speech; this is an architecture for my lived and imaginative experience that had not before been so regally housed.

We live into the spaces we create from our imaginations through consistent diligence.

This past year, as I've taken up the task of writing these weekly essays, I've undone my relationship with my beliefs about myself, my relationship with time, and the possibility and potential of my own actions. It had not been my expectation that I would travel this path when I undertook the journey of this project. I did not expect to see this reflection of myself; I did not set out to arrive at this understanding at the destination of fifty essays on the cusp of this fiftieth birthday.

But that's the remarkable thing about an adventure: the undertaking involves not only risks, but the unknown. On life's journey, the unusual path may yield richness because it is unexpected, because of the way it surprises us and reveals something new. We understand life to be discovery. It is the process of finding information, a place, an object, or a relationship, often for the first time, sometimes again, when we approach with new eyes or awareness. This journey of discovery is the only thing in which we can be manifested and revealed, not only to others and the world, but to ourselves.

But first, we must imagine, intend, and commit, and take the first step of adventure, especially when we don't know, but are curious and open to, whatever it is that we will find.

Afterword

Sometimes it takes an acute experience, even something awful, to get us to pay attention to the journey rather than fixating on the destination.

I began the process of writing these essays in the spring of 2020, a traumatic time for me. I know now that I was never really in danger, but the vigilant posture I assumed during that period drained me emotionally and psychically. Mostly I experienced isolation and sensory deprivation; I was utterly alone and lacked any human contact for months. I was fortunate to work from home, but the days were long and endless, and I woke up exhausted every morning. I was stunned by the sudden deaths of many people I knew, and other friends of mine were in the hospital or suffering debilitating symptoms at home. I felt powerless to help them, and we were all ordered to stay inside. The city where I lived was desolated and further emptying out. And so, I found myself in a funk on my forty-ninth birthday. I mark this day as the nadir of my pandemic experience. There may have been some tears of self-pity that afternoon, until some interior voice told me that I had to get a grip on my situation.

The seed of these essays was planted at that moment. I decided to start journaling, first thing in the morning, for twelve minutes a day as my tea steeped. I figured I might as well do something with my time that would make myself feel better and give me some purpose. What germinated was the idea to write fifty essays over the next year and post these on my private social media as a way of communicating with and staying connected to my friends. The process of writing these essays, the time taken just for me, would be a birthday gift to myself.

Careful readers will notice that fewer than the full complement of the fifty essays I wrote during that year made it into this book. The majority are reproduced with edits to improve clarity and style, but otherwise they reflect the period in which they were written, which means they often reference the events of the pandemic. The essays that didn't make it were too localized in time or place to be understood by anyone but close friends or were simply too personal or self-absorbed to be of interest to anyone but me. Others were cut because they were just not well written and couldn't be salvaged. Even so, this collection reflects the mindful journaling I did during that first pandemic year and my journey of finding my voice as a writer of essays.

Coming back to this collection now, I'm struck by the way these essays reflect the personal changes I underwent during this time. Friends remark that I exited lockdown more confident, less anxious, and with greater wisdom. The period turned out to be very good for me. My life before the pandemic had been full, and I see now, too full. I was so busy I could not catch a moment to be with my own thoughts. The pandemic, with its forced slowdown, brought into focus my relationship with time and helped me clarify what was important to me. As I returned to the page day after day, I confronted my fears and processed difficult emotions, like sadness, anger, and anxiety. I also discovered my resilience as I took a measure of everything I was going through and how I was handling it. I whispered my joys and hopes onto the page and leaned into action to make my dreams come true. I saw reflected to me what was working well, the community supporting me, and the power of my faith. Mindful journaling was healing, expansive, and affirming for me.

It was healing in another way, too. I became more self-aware and confident in myself and my choices. I realized what I valued and how I wanted to spend my time in order to live my life well. As I returned to the page each day, I learned how to acknowledge the responsibility we each have of making hard choices about who we are and how we live out our days. Journaling revealed to me the value in self-discovery through writing and the way that this daily practice can subtly nudge you to set goals and keep you accountable. Mindful journaling helped me rediscover that I really enjoy writing (even when I don't), and I can't live without it. That revelation, and the journey it took me to get there, was the best gift to myself I could have given—and received.

Publishing these essays has also reinforced for me the power of journaling. I have heard from so many readers that the essays contained practical wisdom and insights for their own meditation and writing practice. If there is anything in this book that has made you curious about

starting your own mindful journaling practice, I encourage
you to give it a try. A daily practice of mindful journaling
can relieve anxiety by helping you process thoughts and
challenging emotions, reduce stress by helping you clarify
priorities and your own desires, and improve gratitude
by pulling into focus what you can depend on and enjoy.

Together with this book I have published a Companion
Workbook that you can use for your own journal practice.
Even if you are nervous, if you doubt whether you can
do it, just start with ten minutes a day, or three lines in a
notebook, or whatever works for you. Journaling doesn't
need to look a certain way or use literary language or be
readable to anyone but you. Just start. And stick with it.
If you fall off the practice for a bit, pick it up again when
you can. Journaling, like the best things in life, is a practice
of commitment, of showing up. Remember: the journey's
the thing.

As for me, I continue to journal. I have learned that the
practice of witnessing my own thoughts and processing my
own feelings with compassion and detachment has become
my motivation for living my life fully and with purpose.
If this book moves you to pick up a pen or put fingers to
keyboard and begin your own journey, then sharing my
own story was worth the vulnerability.

Discussion and
Reflection Questions

Although the author journaled alone, she writes that she shared her journal entries as weekly essays with a small group of friends on social media, and these led to conversations that sustained her and helped her refine her ideas and grow.

This is your invitation to find a community to share your reactions to the essays in this book and your own ideas about the topics. Use the questions below to frame your conversations.

If it's helpful, the questions can also serve as prompts to your own journaling and to guide your reflection on the topics and themes in the book.

1. This is a book of essays that resulted from a year in which the author journaled every day for at least twelve minutes a day. Why did she start this project? What did she expect to accomplish? What actually happened?

2. This author wrote this book during a period of stress and trauma for her. The book starts in the early days of the pandemic in 2020 and records the author's

experience of a time that most people would rather forget. How does she come to terms with what is happening in the world and how it affects her personally? How does reading about the pandemic now make you feel? Can you relate your experiences?

3. New York City is an important character in these essays. What role does that city play in this book and in the author's life? How was it similar or different to your local experience?

4. Each week the author picks a word and meditates on it in an essay. Which essays inspired you the most, and why?

5. How does the author's relationship to writing change throughout the year? What does she learn from the consistent work she puts into writing?

6. The author experiences writer's block several times. How does she handle these experiences to keep writing? How do you navigate what holds you back?

7. The author comes to a new understanding of a favorite childhood book, *The Little Prince*, as an adult. How does she experience this book now, and what does it teach her about growth? Have you had a similar experience when you have returned to an important book or movie from your childhood?

8. There are several essays in which the author meditates on the feelings of home and of belonging. The author talks about moving, growing up in an unstable home, and emigrating as an adult back to her own country. What is home for you?

9. In "On What I Haven't Done," she states: "I want to live in a world of hard attention." What do you think she means?

10. In "On Deciding," the author wrestles with the relationship of fear and inaction. What do you make of her advice to "choose the right size of fear"?

11. In the essay "On Courage," she describes courage as an act of character, of acting despite being afraid. In "On Cowardice," the author relates courage to planning and intentionality as ways of bypassing fear. How do you understand courage and cowardice?

12. "On Faith" celebrates the author's hero Terry Fox. Why does the author admire this person? What role do heroes play in our lives? Who are your heroes, and why?

13. "Trust cannot be passive...[it] must be acted upon," the author declares in "On Faith." Does this ring true to you? What does faith mean to you? How do you demonstrate how you place your faith?

14. In the essay "On Exhaustion," we see the author

surrender, and "On Grace" hints at the author's beating heart and her vulnerabilities. When does surrender become an act of power and grace?

15. A few things belonging to the author are destroyed during the year, including a glass vase and a beloved coffee pot. The author also returns to the theme of loss and grief many times including in "On Mourning." What role does grief play in your everyday life?

16. The author is isolated for most of the year, but she writes often about other people. How do you stay connected to people that matter most to you?

17. In which essay does the author make her prescription for a good life, a life worth living, most clear? Do you agree? What does "a good life" mean to you?

Acknowledgments

Writing these essays has shown me that so much joy is possible with the discipline of consistency plus the help of momentum and community. I dedicate these pages to all those who accompanied me, directly and indirectly, in the generation of this book.

Before I started writing again, I was working through my thoughts and feelings by running, and it helped me to meet great people. The myth of the solo runner is just that, a myth. Running is a team sport, and I am grateful for my core running community, which is a foundation of my life in New York City. I would like to thank coaches Stuart, Dara, Craig, Duncan, John, Paul, and Steph, and members of my run group who have listened to my meditations on so many of the topics in these pages: David, Corrie, Mark, Carol, Janet, Heather and Steve, Rebecca and Cooke, Francesca, Ghassan, Rami, Maria, John, Andrea, Celeste, Claudia, Jerri, Kumiko, Rosemary, RoseMary, Bijay, and Tara. And, of course, gratitude to the two other members of my long run Three Amigos, Michael and Lewis. You have both helped me through some very long miles and longer conversations.

Thanks, too, to my social media community that engaged with these essays as they were first being produced.

I am grateful to everyone who liked, loved, left comments, or otherwise interacted with any or all these musings. Your desire that I turn this into something you can share has resulted in this reworked little packet of words. Special thanks to Winsome, Doug, Kelly, Jodi, Tudor, Julian, Melissa, and Dhriti for your early readership and feedback.

There should be a special place of comfort and joy for those who inspired me to write at all and then to edit and publish these essays, including Valerie and Ari, Tony, Brian, Janice, and Joy. I am grateful to my New York muses, Gretl and Laura, and my Toronto crew, including Cathy, Paula, Dina, Jenn B., and Sharon G., all of whom continue to remain connected despite distance. I am thankful for Robi and her kick in the pants. My New York City Writers' Group, Victor, Donna, Bridget, and Peter, encouraged me to publish and showed me the way. Billy B. was a catalyst and a thorn to getting the audiobook out. I take so much pleasure in the continuation of Video Book Club, because they are awesome and because they keep me in fiction: Allison, Penelope, Mathilda, Emily, Adriana, Antonia, and Anastasia (and Chris)—thank you. I am delighted that I was able to deepen my relationship with my cousin Robin during our semi-frequent chats over wine during the period I was writing these essays. Many of the ideas in these essays sprang from our conversations.

Every published writer has a red-ribbon list of those whose contributions to the finished product are outsized. Enormous gratitude to Gail C., who got me writing again as an adult and who has consistently been a ferocious cheerleader. Sharon G.'s friendship is legendary, and she has been my "reality check" reader, whose comments and support have moved the reality of publishing this book forward. Peter endured endless questions about certain edits and clarified my thinking. Heather enabled me to record the audiobook with minimal drama and maximal animal company. Michael established Quentin Imprints and continues to serve as a sounding board and inspiration across the complexity of my life and its happenings, all the while dragging me through runs around Central Park. And my heart remains full of instruction and constructive criticism from my high-school English teacher, Scott Baker, whose early belief in me remains my touchstone during writing blocks: Even though I haven't seen you in thirty years, I finally hear you and understand.

Steacy, the family I chose and the world's greatest little sister, is both the star of and catalyst for these pages. I love everything about you, and I am so proud of you.

And to mum and dad, my first and forever readers: I love you "to the mars!" and across the whole of the solar system. I am so grateful you both got to read these essays in draft as they were initially released. I will always be your wise little owl, and your dictionary borrower-in-chief. Rest in peace.

About the Author

PHOTOGRAPH BY GIANCARLO OSABEN

Dera Nevin began keeping a diary at the age of nine. Born into an unconventional family, she learned to process her emotions and make sense of the world around her by writing. As a teen and young adult, she wrote a play, poems, and short stories, some of which won awards.

As an adult, she had the opportunity to go to law school and then practiced law for two decades. After several busy and difficult years in a row, during which she was confronted by multiple work, health, and family challenges, Dera started journaling off and on again. Then during the pandemic year of 2020, she recommitted to a consistent daily journal practice of at least twelve minutes a day. The practice left her calmer, more focused, and energized, and she found renewed purpose in her writing. As she started to share her journal entries once a week on social media, she realized that her journal prompting techniques were inspiring to those around her. Dera is now the founder of Quentin Imprints LLC, a company dedicated to personal discovery and expression.

Dera enjoys running, reading, exploring New York City, watching the performing arts, and traveling, all of which are frequent topics in her journaling. Her New York City apartment is crammed with books, plants, and running shoes. *The Journey's the Thing* is her first book.

You can connect with Dera on social media and at www.deranevin.com.